The Book on Internet Marketing for Pool and Spa Dealers

How to Outsmart, Out Market and Outsell Your Competition in 90 Days or Less

Includes New Post Pandemic Marketing Strategies

David Carleton
www.SpaPoolMarketingSuccess.com

The Book on Internet Marketing for Pool and Spa Dealers
Copyright 2019, 2022 by David Carleton

Disclaimer
This book is designed to provide information regarding the subject matter covered. It is sold with the understanding that the publisher and authors and advisers are not rendering legal, accounting, or other professional services. The information provided is on an "as is" basis.

The authors, publishers and advisors shall have neither liability nor responsibility to any person(s) or entity of any kind with respect to any loss or damage caused or alleged to be caused directly or indirectly from or arising as a result of the information contained in this manual. What you are about to read are the ideas, opinions, thoughts, and ideas express only by the author.

Every effort has been made to make this manual as complete and as accurate as possible. However, there may be mistakes both typographical and in content. Therefore, this text should be used only as a general guide and not as the ultimate source of Internet marketing. Furthermore, this manual contains information only up to the printing date.

Table of Contents

Introduction – Why You Need This Book

Congratulations on taking a critical step towards ensuring the future success of your business. Just by investing in this book, you are way ahead of any local competitors who didn't know this information was available or simply chose to ignore it.

By the time you finish reading this book; you will have significantly increased your chances of surviving and even thriving in any type of economy.

The reason I decided to write this book was to help as many dealers as I can that I know are struggling to increase their sales and profits.

During my dealer consultations, I usually get asked the same 5 questions…

- How can I increase sales?
- How can I improve my closing ratio?
- How do I attract more potential customers?
- How should I allocate my advertising budget?
- What can I do that will have the most immediate impact on my business?

All these questions will be addressed in the book

Stop Using Old Strategies to Generate New Business

In my opinion, our industry is at a true crossroads. Manufacturer consolidation, shrinking dealer base and fewer buyers in the market with less money to spend - all of these have taken their toll.

And with some owners "giving away the farm" just to generate cash flow, dealers are spending even more time with prospects justifying the value of their products and services.

The bright spot is, you're still in business. So, congratulations, you have weathered hopefully the worst part. But in order to survive and thrive going forward, you better be prepared to change the way you do business.

It's time to stop using old strategies to generate new business.

And hoping for the best is not a strategy, waiting it out is just not possible and ignoring new ideas is no longer an option! So please…keep an open mind, be receptive to some new ideas and most importantly…be ready to… take action.

But first, who am I and why should you listen to me? Good question! First and foremost, I am a devoted husband and the proud father of 3 great children. My work experience comes from having held 20 different positions in sales, marketing, and general management for many well-known consumer goods companies.

My pool and spa industry experience come from 6 years at Dimension One Spas where I was Vice President of Sales and Marketing. While in that position, I developed sales, marketing and training programs that helped hundreds of dealers in 30 countries around the world generate leads, increase sales, and enhance their marketing effectiveness.

In 2007, I left Dimension One to start my own marketing consulting company. Yeah, I know, great time to start a business, but here I am years later running a successful company helping others do the same.

In addition to my consulting business, I have written books on Lead Generation, Referral Marketing and Social Media and have spoken at several industry trade shows and conventions. I have also been featured on several prominent news shows and many newspapers, and magazines across the USA including SpaRetailer where I am a contributing writer.

OK, enough about me, let's get started…

Industry Research for Context.
According to a SpaRetailer Magazine survey, 88% of spa buyers shop at least 3 brands before purchasing and 92% of spa buyers research the brand online before visiting a store! Let me repeat that...9 out of 10 spa buyers go ONLINE BEFORE they visit a store!

All this information points to one conclusion...Internet marketing is critical to your business. If you choose to ignore these facts, then I can assure you that your business won't be here in a few years! Blunt? Yes. Harsh? Maybe. Reality? Absolutely!

The Bottom Line is That You Need to:

- Show up consistently on page #1 of the search engines
- Have an informative website that generates leads
- Give prospects a reason to "like" you and trust you
- Educate prospects on why your dealership and products are better than the competition and
- Follow up religiously with prospects after they leave your website

And of course, you must do all this BETTER than your local competitors!

So, if you're struggling, what are you doing wrong and what do you need to do to fix it? Either you're not doing the right things or you're doing the right things the wrong way. The purpose of this book is to point you in the right direction. It's a wake-up call to focus your attention on working smarter, not harder!

The Dynamics of the Pool and Spa Industry Has Changed.
As I'm sure you've already discovered, it now takes more than your typical newspaper ad, radio spot and weekend home show to get the sales you used to get. Why? Because the dynamics of the spa and pool market have changed dramatically. Consumers are more cautious than ever and are doing more research to be sure they are getting the best products and services at the best possible price.

And where are they going to do their research? You guessed it...the Internet. If you think that just having a website is enough, you are sadly mistaken. You obviously need your website to be FOUND by your prospects.

But, according to some studies, 90% of people searching for products and services on the Internet never search beyond page one. Take a moment to think about how many times you search for something on Google and how many times you actually go past page one during your search. If you're like most, not too many times.

That means that for all practical purposes, if you're not on page one, your prospects will never find you! And if they can't find you, they can't buy from you either. To make matters worse, look at all the time, money, and resources you've already spent creating that beautiful website that 90% of your potential clients and customers will never see. How frustrating!

You already know how important marketing is to the success of your business, but if you're only using the traditional "offline" marketing and lead generation strategies, then you're working twice as hard for half the results. That's why it's critical to start continually improving your Internet marketing.

The 9 Steps to Internet Marketing Success – Overview

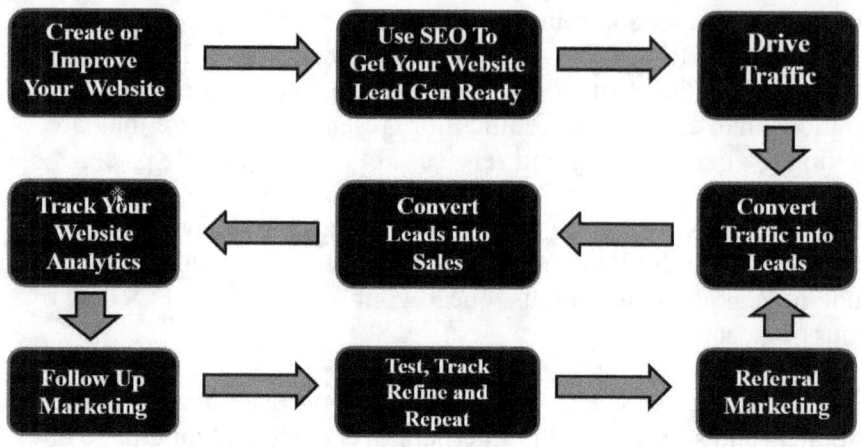

This section of the book is a quick introduction and overview of my 9 Steps to Internet Marketing Success for Pool and Spa Dealers. It's what I discuss with all prospective clients because it follows a successful formula that I developed over the last 35 years and has been implemented successfully by hundreds of dealers across the world to drive more traffic, generate more leads and ultimately increase sales.

Each of the 9 steps listed below has a chapter devoted to it, which goes into the specific strategies I recommend that you implement. I highly recommend that you not skip ahead to a specific chapter but follow the 9 steps "in order." Doing so will ensure you get the maximum value from the book and help improve your chances of significantly growing your business.

Step 1 - Create or Improve Your Website.
It's hard to believe, but yes, some dealers still don't have their own website. If you are one of them, I can almost guarantee that no matter how successful you are today, without a website, your days are numbered. Sorry to be so blunt, but that's the reality.

Hire a good website designer and you can have a basic site up in less than a week. And please, don't have your son's high school friend create the site. Hire a professional who knows as much about business as they do about websites. You never get a second chance to make a first impression, so spend a little more and get it done right.

Step 2 – Use On-Site SEO to Get Your Website Lead Generation Ready.
There is no point in building a website unless you can attract visitors. The biggest source of traffic for most websites are search engines like Google, Yahoo and MSN (Bing). SEO or search engine optimization is a strategy used to improve the on-site or on-page content and coding of your website in order to become more relevant to the search engines for your niche and keywords.

Implementing on-site SEO strategies will help increase visitor traffic because your site will rank higher in the Search Engine Results Pages (SERPS).

Ongoing strategic and effective search engine optimization can continually improve your rankings month after month, year after year. SEO will help you achieve long lasting search engine ranking status because your listing appears in the "natural" or "organic" listings where 70+/-% of all the clicks take place.

Step 3 - Drive Qualified Traffic to Your Website.
There are many ways to drive traffic to your website, some cost you little in terms of actual cash, while others are more sophisticated and complicated and will need to be budgeted. We'll review a variety of specific strategies in the next few chapters.

Step 4 - Convert Website Visitors into Leads.
Everything you do on your website should have one overriding objective – turning visitors into leads and ultimately leads into sales! The only way to verifiably do this is to capture their contact information of choice.

Website "surfers" behave rather impulsively on the Internet, so much so that many times they easily forget where they were even a few website pages/clicks ago. That's why it is so critical to convert as many first-time visitors as possible...and quickly!

And the best way to convert a visitor to a lead is by offering some useful information or something of value that will help a prospective buyer make an informed buying decision. Buyer's guides, surveys, brochures, product selection, pricing or even free in-home consultations are just a few ways to do this.

Step 5 - Covert Leads into Sales.
Now that you have a lead and have delivered the information that was requested, how do you follow up? Many/most times it is the job of your sales team to follow up with prospects. Typical follow up methods include e-mail, phone call, newsletters, text/message/chat, direct mail, or some combination of a few of these.

Some experts say that it takes between 5 and 12 contacts before a prospect begins to trust you and what you are selling. Leaving it to memory to do this follow up is a recipe for failure. You must implement an automated and systemized method to stay in touch.

Step 6 - Track Your Results Using Analytics & Continually Improve.
Analyzing your web traffic statistics can be an invaluable tool for making critical sales, marketing, and budgeting decisions. The aim is to use your website's analytics to figure out how well your site is working for you and your visitors.

Website stats can help you determine how effective and engaging important pages and sections of your website are, which keywords visitors used to find you, where they went when they got to your site and how much time they actually spend on each page and so much more. Knowing this type of information is essential information to any successful business, website, and Internet marketing strategy.

Step 7 - Create a Follow Up Marketing System.
As previously mentioned, once you get website visitors to "opt-in" they want and expect you to send them information and offerings. There are many ways you can follow up with a prospect and the best way sometimes depends on how they've requested the follow up – phone, e-mail, chat, text, in person, etc.

A great way to stay in touch with all your current customers and prospects is by sending out e-newsletters because it builds long lasting relationships that foster trust and trust that makes you money. In addition, it keeps you top of mind (TOM), so you're the first person your e-mail list members think of next time they want or need what any of your products and services.

Step 8 - Test, Track, Refine, Repeat.
Testing what's working and what's not, shouldn't be just a one-time occurrence. This is something you should be doing constantly, always trying to improve your previous results. This could mean a website headline, an e-mail subject line, an AdWords campaign, a direct mail piece, social media posting, YouTube video, etc.
When you do decide to test a specific strategy, be sure not to test too many variables at one time. Even though your changes might have given you improved results, testing too many at one time will not tell you which change resulted in the improvement.

Step 9 - Create a Referral Marketing System.
You know what happens with many dealers after a prospect finally does become a customer, not much! Many times, they are all but ignored in terms of marketing time, money, and resources. As small business owners, we are so conditioned to closing the next deal that we often forget what a great resource our current customer base is!

Seriously, think about your own business – do you have a referral marketing SYSTEM and budget in place right now? And remember, word-of-mouth is not a system! Most dealers don't have a systemized method of getting referrals and that is a missed opportunity to increase your sales and profits.

So, there you have it - your 9 steps to spa and pool dealer Internet marketing success.

From this point forward, be prepared to read practical advice and strategies learned from years of trial and error and constant testing and refinement.

You will notice the content in this book is a combination of several different writing styles including:

- Article style with a lot of details
- Bullet point overviews
- Checklists for quick reading

It is written this way because not every section requires a detailed explanation while I felt other sections needed more information to explain the strategy. Regardless of which section you're reading or which style you like better, I promise you'll find all the information helpful to grow your business.

Now, let's review all these steps in much more detail.

Step 1

Create or Improve Your Website

In most cases, your website is the first contact a potential client or customer has with you or your company. It doesn't matter what type of products you sell; your website is your silent salesperson.

And just like any first-time face-to-face meeting, you never get a second chance to make a first impression. Said another way - your website must WOW visitors, persuade them to want to learn more about your products and services and compel them to act.

Sound easy? With more options available to consumers than ever before, and the average attention span equal to a goldfish (9 seconds), most people searching the Internet for information are not easily impressed. So, building and maintaining a high performing business website is critical. Step one is to ensure that when visitors arrive at your website, they have the best experience possible.

In this chapter, we'll look at a few simple things you can do to your website to improve the user experience (UX).

The Purpose of Your Website

Other than providing the opportunity for consumers and prospects to find you online, the main purpose of your website is threefold:

1. **POSITION** you and your business as an industry expert - the one best source for all your products and services.
2. **EDUCATE** and inform potential customers about why they should buy from you, and most importantly...

3. **CONVERT** website visitors into high quality leads.

These three actions - POSITION, EDUCATE and CONVERT - lay out the simple, but effective strategy behind every successful business website. Remember, all things being equal, people will always buy at the lowest price. So, you need a great website to educate them on why they should take the next step to contact you.

Not convinced? Here's a perfect example. During a recent Chamber of Commerce presentation, I asked if there were any real estate agents in the room. A woman in the back raised her hand. I asked her what she would do for me if I gave her my listing. After thinking for a moment, she shared how she would create a comprehensive marketing plan including an MLS listing, advertising, open houses, and roadway signage.

I thanked her for her answer and asked if there were any other agents in the room. A gentleman raised his hand. When I asked him if he would do all the things the other agent promised, he said yes. Then I asked him if he'd be willing to drop his listing fee from 6% (the other agent's commission) to 5% to get my business and he confirmed that he would.

If both agents were willing to do the exact same thing for me, then why would I want to pay more for the first agent? The bottom line? If you fail to differentiate yourself from your competition, then buyers will make purchasing decisions based on price alone. So, what differentiates you? Your unique selling proposition (USP).

Develop a Unique Selling Proposition (USP)

A USP is what sets your business apart from the competition. It's what makes you different and why prospects should do business with you.

To develop your USP you need to look at what problems your prospective customers have and how your company can solve these problems better than anybody else.

Here are some typical concerns and complaints prospective buyers have in the pool and spa industry:

- Spas are hard to maintain.
- I have to use too many chemicals.
- Pools cost a lot to operate.
- What happens if I buy the wrong spa?
- What happens if I want to move my hot tub?

Regardless of what product or service you sell, think about the questions your customers ask daily. Are these questions being answered on your website, so people have what they need to take the next step?

Performance Gap Method.
One easy way to determine your USP is to use the "Performance Gap Method." To start, identify the problems your current or prospective customers have and what you and your competitors offer as solutions. The difference between the two is your opportunity. Put another way, the gap that exists between known industry problems and the solution your biggest competitor offers creates an opportunity to improve your USP.

Industry Problems - Competitor Offering = Your Opportunity

However, not everything your competition overlooks constitutes an opportunity. Here are a few poor USP examples:

- Service with a smile
- Good quality at affordable prices
- We'll beat any competitor's price
- Satisfaction guaranteed

While all the points mentioned above are important, saying or doing them probably won't set you apart from your competition. Now, consider a few ideas that might.

- Onsite training and assistance

- 24-hour service
- One free drain and refill after 6 months

Another great example of a high value USP is a money-back guarantee. Imagine that you sell a product to someone for $10,000 and it includes a 30-day money-back guarantee. This would certainly make you stand out from your competition and would likely make your customer feel more comfortable purchasing from you.

Optimize Your Website Design

There are many steps involved in creating a new website, and great books are available on how to go about doing this on your own. This section of this book is not intended to be a comprehensive "deep dive" into website design. Rather, it aims to highlight the strategic decisions you need to make and specific direction you need to communicate to the person or agency you've selected to build your website.

Caution! Hiring an expert to design your business website is smart. But the following information is important for you to read and understand. Why? Even if someone else is crafting your website, the direction you provide affects the look and feel of your site and the end user experience - which we know from reading above ultimately impacts how many leads you generate. This information comes from testing, researching, and building hundreds of websites over the last 15 years.

Full Screen vs. Boxed Screen Website Design.
A full screen design appears when someone lands on your website and what they see takes up the entire width of the computer screen. In full screen layout, there are common elements like menu columns and sidebars that are the same width.

By comparison, a boxed design is contained within a vertical box centered in the middle of the computer screen with either a colored background or image "behind" it. A boxed screen ensures that the layout is always the same, regardless of screen size. Both full screen and boxed screen designs can be responsive websites.

Long Scrolling vs. 'Above the Fold' Homepage.
With a long scrolling homepage, visitors need to continuously scroll on their device to see everything on the webpage. With an 'above the fold' homepage, it's not necessary to scroll as everything shows at once on the screen.

'Above the fold' is an old newspaper term that refers to the upper half of the front page of a newspaper or tabloid. This is generally where the most important news stories or photographs are located (Wikipedia).

Long scrolling has some unique benefits. And, despite having to continuously scroll to find information, people don't seem to mind. Just think about the popularity of Facebook and Twitter – a huge user base proves that people are happy to scroll, even on a mobile device.

On the other hand, analyzing website analytics can be complicated with a long scroll homepage. For example, achieving a low bounce rate is tough as people tend to drop off when they must scroll through too much information or wait for large photos and images to load. I've added heatmaps to dozens of websites over the years, and discovered this: people will scroll, but most don't like to scroll very far.

Long Scrolling: Pros and Cons

Pros:
- Faster & more convenient than clicking.
- Easy to view information quickly without page load time interfering.
- Non-committal and doesn't require the user to make a decision via a selected click.

- People are used to scrolling on mobile devices.

Cons:
- Can feel cumbersome and never-ending.
- Lengthy pages can create disinterest.
- Content can get confusing if information doesn't flow logically.
- Tougher to track specific website analytics.

Above the Fold: Pros and Cons

Pros:
- Users can "find what they are looking for faster`.
- Clearly organized, easy to see everything without having to scroll.
- Tracking for analytics is much easier.

Cons:
- Users need to make conscious decisions about how and where to navigate.
- Clicking is a committed action; unwilling visitors may leave the site.
- Long load times can interrupt flow, decreasing user experience.

Website Sliders.
Generally, I am not a big fan of sliders for the following reasons:

- Studies show that sliders do not help conversions.
- Sliders have low click-through rates. (Leadpages.com)
- Sliders aren't often mobile-friendly.
- Sliders can hurt your SEO - If the sliders are loading slow, then people may just hit the back button.

Timing

Show sliders too fast and your visitors will have a hard time reading what's there. Show them too slow and your visitors are not likely to wait around to see them all.

Calls to Action (CTAs) on Sliders

CTAs can be effective on sliders, but there's a catch. If you do have sliders, don't just put the calls to action on the sliders. Other than the first slider, most will never be seen. While sales promotions or special offers are fine on sliders, few people ever make it to the 5th or 6th slider because they've already started clicking somewhere on the homepage, which sends them to a different page on your site.

Mobile Friendly Design is a Must (Responsive vs. Unique).
Look at your traffic stats on Google Analytics and you'll probably notice more and more traffic coming from mobile devices like smart phones or tablets. I've seen increases of 30% to 50% year over year from mobile - all at the expense of traditional desktop computers. And it's only going to continue to increase.

Mobile Stats to Consider
- 91% of Americans own a cell phone of some kind *
- 79% of smartphone users have their phone on or near them for all but two hours of their waking day**

When people use mobile devices *to search for products and services they are:* ***
- 39% more likely to call a business
- 57% more likely to visit the store
- 51% more likely to make a purchase

* https://www.pewresearch.org/internet/fact-sheet/mobile/
** https://www.adweek.com/digital/smartphones/
*** https://www.thinkwithgoogle.com/marketing-resources/micro-moments/connecting-the-dots-measuring-your-micromoments-strategy/

With mobile web design, I like to separate mobile websites into 3 options.

1. *No Mobile Website.* A "no mobile site" looks exactly like a mini version of the main site. This means everything is very small, hard to read and therefore it's pretty much worthless.

2. *Responsive Website.* Responsive means that your website design is mobile-friendly. On a mobile device, a responsive site takes all the content on a page (text, photos, videos, etc.) and stacks it vertically to be displayed on any size screen. Users only need to scroll to see everything on the page.

   Since the "stacking" process is automatic, you can't control how it stacks. So, if you want to move text, a headline, or a photo to a different spot on a mobile device, you must change where or how it appears on a desktop device. Sometimes, trying to accommodate your mobile device preferences changes how the desktop version appears.

3. *Plugins for WordPress/Drupal Type Website.* There are many free and paid mobile device plugins available. Most create a single landing page made up of the major navigation tabs that allow users to get where they want to go without scrolling. The better plugins also have a "click to call" feature for easy one-touch calling.

   One thing to note when using a plugin is that they are mostly used to create a homepage. After the user clicks on a link, they will usually end up on a normal desktop version of the page. But plugins can get visitors where they want to go much faster than scrolling.

A Word About Google Mobile Friendly vs. Consumer Friendly.
If you want to see if your mobile site is Google friendly, type it into this Google URL: **https://search.google.com/test/mobile-friendly**. After a few seconds, you'll find out if Google considers your site mobile friendly.

Remember, 'Google friendly' doesn't necessarily mean 'consumer friendly'. Your mobile site may be technically mobile friendly, but that doesn't mean it provides a good user experience. I like to use the one-page plugin option whenever possible because I think it's more user friendly.

Website Best Practices

Technical.
1. Ensure Your Website Uses Https vs. Http.
> According to Google*, you should always protect all your websites with HTTPS, even if they
> don't handle sensitive communications. Aside from providing critical security and data integrity for
> both your websites and your users' personal information, HTTPS is a requirement for many new browser features, particularly those required for progressive web apps.

> And, according to Search Engine Land**, effective July 2018, Google's Chrome browser will mark
> non-HTTPS sites as "not secure." After years of pushing for 'secure by default' websites, Google will identify insecure sites in the Chrome browser beginning mid-summer. There are more details available on this, but for now, simply tell your webmaster that your site needs to be https.

2. Get Visitors Where They Need to Go in the Fewest Number of Clicks.
> We've already discussed this in terms of homepage design and navigation tabs, but if you check the *Visitor Flow* section of your Google Analytics, you will see how visitors to your site click and drop off after each click. This is an eye-opening activity and will hopefully encourage you to remove unnecessary pages from your website.

3. Ensure all Call to Actions, Alerts and Leads are Sent to You.
> Leads should go to a trusted person in your organization who is responsible for following up in a timely and professional

manner. Leads should NOT go to your web developer or marketing agency!

*https://developers.google.com/web/fundamentals/security/encrypt-in-transit/why-https
**https://searchengineland.com/effective-july-2018-googles-chrome-browser-will-mark-non-https-sites-as-not-secure-291623

Content.

1. Make Your Homepage Count.

A well-conceived homepage is critical to the success of the entire user experience on a website. Even small changes to the homepage can have a major impact. Think of your website's homepage like the table of contents of a book - a quick summary of what's inside. *The faster you can get people off your homepage and deeper into your site, the faster you will make money.*

Not only is a well-designed homepage better for your site visitors, but it also reduces your "bounce rate" as measured by Google Analytics. A high bounce rate means someone arrived at a page on your website and left from the same page. They did not click and go to another page. So, if you want people to go to a specific product page or to request a price quote or free buyer's guide, then make sure the link is prominent on the homepage.

2. Use Short vs. Long Paragraphs.

When writing online content for websites, it's best to break up paragraphs into two or three sentence paragraphs. Sure, some grammar experts will disagree, but this creates necessary white space. The extra room not only makes your text much easier to read, but also provides the reader with a better user experience. You can also bold titles to make it easy for people to search for specific information.

3. Include Your Phone Number and Address on Every Page.

Often, people come to your site just to get your phone number or to see where you're located. Don't make them search for this information. Have it readily available on every page. Remember, the harder you make your website visitors work, the less likely they are to take the action you want. Don't make potential buyers scroll all the way to the bottom to find your contact information. Make it easy for them to find your business and contact you by phone.

4. *Create a Unique and Informational 404 Error Page.*
A 404 error-page appears when a user types in a direct link to a page that does not exist on your site. It can also happen if you have internal links on your site that go to a page that no longer exists. This is common website language, that simply says, "That page does not exist".

If you fail to create your own 404 error page, one of two things will happen: either your website theme will show a very bland message or worse, the search engine will show some sort of message. Neither option is good. Ask your webmaster to create a unique and informative 404 error page that explains why the user is getting this message and where they should go to find the information they are looking for.

Strategy Behind Webpages.
1. *Ensure Each Page Has a Purpose.*
You started out with a new website that had 25 relevant pages. "Suddenly," five years later, your website now has 50 pages. Over time, you may have added or changed models, product lines, promotions, videos, etc. and the older pages weren't removed. I suggest you review all the pages on your site though the eyes of a new website visitor. Is each page helpful? Does it add value? If not, get rid of it.

2. *Ensure Each Page Has a "Most Wanted Response".*
When someone comes to your website's homepage, what do you want them to do? Most people say, "Well, I want them to call me." Okay, valid answer. So, does your phone number appear on the homepage? How easy is it to find? Is at the top

or is at the bottom? Is it clickable on a mobile device? Is that all you want website visitors to do?

Start thinking like a prospect who doesn't always want to call you. If you want people to contact you, then you need to provide them with options THEY want to use, not just the ones YOU want. That means making it easy for them to contact you by email, phone, text, chat, Facebook messenger, and even in person.

3. *Add Badges to Improve Your Trust Factor.*
One of the best ways to build trust and credibility is through icons or badges that appear on your website. Specific badges show your business is certified, approved, and highly rated from trade organizations like the Better Business Bureau (BBB), HomeAdvisor, SpaRetailer. etc. Social media icons are also considered a trust factor.

4. *Include a "Home" Tab on Your Navigation Bar.*
Most web savvy visitors know that when you click an online logo on a website, you return to the homepage. But not every visitor knows this. Always include a "home" navigation tab at the top of your site.

5. *Minimize Navigation Drop-Down Menus Whenever Possible.*
The goal is to get your website visitors where they want to go as quickly as possible and with the fewest number of clicks. So, organizing and prioritizing drop-down menus is highly recommended.

6. *Ensure all the Links on Your Site Work.*
There are several free services that you can use to ensure your website links are all in working order. Start by Googling "Free Broken Link Checker."

Look & Feel

1. Check the Spelling and Grammar on Your Entire Site.
It's embarrassing to get emails from clients telling you that you've mis-spelled something.

2. Review Color Combinations for Easy Reading.
Make sure the text color is readable on your site background color. Black/grey text on a white background is safe and very easy to read.

"Must Have" Pages for Your Website

About Us.
Would you buy a $5,000 - $30,000 hot tub from a company that you knew nothing about? I wouldn't! That's why you need an "About Us" page. This page should at least contain a short paragraph about the people, products, and mission of the company. Other things to consider adding include photos of your stores, team, fleet of trucks, awards won, societies you belong to, etc.

Contact Us.
Having your name and address on the homepage or in the header is great, but it's not enough. You need a "Contact Us" page where visitors can go, type in their name and email, and ask you a question.

Privacy Policy.
Does your site have a privacy policy? Visitors may not care about a privacy policy, but Google does. More importantly, in order to advertise on Facebook, you need to provide them with a link to your privacy policy. Having a privacy policy page on your website also helps improve the quality score in Google AdWords.

Reviews & Testimonials.
Having reviews on your website that people can read is another key element for building trust. There are systems that can import your company's reviews from Facebook, Google My Business (GMB) and BBB, and consolidate them on one page for your site.

This is helpful to consumers, who don't need to leave your site to see reviews. I'll go into more detail about the reviews system I recommend in a later chapter (**Dealer Automated Reviews System – https://DealerAutomatedReviewsSystem.com**).

Specials & Promotions.

If you don't have a page dedicated to current promotions, I highly recommend that you create one. This will be one of the most visited pages on your site because everyone looking for your products and services wants to save money. After creating this page, be sure that it is always up to date - make sure to remove outdated promotions.

Location Pages.

If you have more than one store or location, it's a good idea to create a separate page for each store. This is mostly for SEO purposes, and you can easily optimize each page for the geography they serve. In addition, you can use newly created location URLs for directories like Google My Business (GMB), Yelp, Facebook, and other social media sites.

Blog.

I highly recommend you have a blog on your website. It's great for providing fresh content for Google and your customers and prospects. But one caveat here - if you have a blog, use it. The last blog entry on your blog shouldn't be several years old. Keep the content fresh and all your blogs should not be about sales and promotions.

There are a variety of non-sale related topics you can write about – see what your competitors or suppliers in your market are blogging about to get some ideas. If you don't want to write your own blogs, have someone else in your company write them for you or hire an industry knowledgeable person or agency.

Things You Should Never Do on Your Website

Never Send Traffic Away from Your Site.
Generally speaking, you never want to send visitors away from your website. You've spent a lot of time, money, and resources to attract website visitors, the last thing you want to do is send them away, as they may never come back! An important exception is when asking visitors to leave a review on sites like Google or Facebook.

How does a website inadvertently send visitors away? Some provide links to partner websites, or offsite resources, like credit applications or vendor sites. Before deciding to add an external link, ask yourself how important these off-site links are and how they help you grow your business.

Here are two ways to provide your visitors access to external information without sending them away.

1. Have a clickable link open a new page, keeping the original page live and visible in their browser. This way, when your visitors exit the "linked page", your original website page is still there. Here is the code:
    `<a href="https://WEBURL.com" target="_blank">Text the You Want Visitors to See</a>`

2. Include the information in an "iFrame". This way, the contents of one website appear as a page right within your own website. Ask your webmaster if this is an option for your website.

Never Use Splash Pages or "Welcome to Our Site" or "Click Here to Enter".
You only get so many clicks out of a prospect when they come to your site. Don't waste them on splash pages that say, "Welcome to our site or "Click here to enter".

Never Add a Newsletter Signup Form if You Don't Publish Anything, it Frustrates Consumers.
People generally aren't looking to get more newsletters in their inbox. However, if you do offer this option, then by all means send out a newsletter. If someone takes the time to opt in, it means they really do want to hear from you.

Website Related 'Must Haves' for Business Owners

Know Who Owns Your Domain Name (Website URL).
I can't tell you how many times I've spoken to dealers that don't know who owns their domain name, where it is registered, when it expires and how or where to log in to find all this information.

Remember this…whoever owns the registration to your domain name ultimately controls your website. If someone other than yourself owns your domain name and that person gets mad at you, they can easily shut your entire website down. **You need to own your domain name.** This is non-negotiable. So, check out who owns yours and make sure you have access to it.

"How do I know who owns my domain name?" Type this into your browser **www.who.godaddy.com**. Then, type your domain name into the space provided and click enter. The results will give you all the information you need to know about who owns your domain, when it expires and where your website is hosted.

Obtain Admin Level Access to Your Website, Hosting & Registrar.
You need to have the highest-level access to your website and hosting service even if someone else manages all this for you. This ensures no one can ever lock you out of your own website and hosting.

You should also have complete control of your domain registration – your domain registrar. Examples of domain registrars are sites like GoDaddy and Network Solutions. There are many others, so be sure you know yours.

Make Sure Google Analytics is Enabled on Your Website.
You can't improve what you can't measure. Google Analytics is free software that you can easily add to your website to give you detailed information about how much traffic comes to your site, how long visitors stay and what pages they click on. There is an entire chapter dedicated to Google Analytics later in this book. But for now, be sure you have it on your site and that you have full admin access.

Set up Google Search Console.
Google Search Console provides an even more detailed look at your website stats than Google Analytics and is also a free service provided by Google. More about Search Console in a future chapter.

Prioritize Site Security.
Websites built using WordPress, Drupal and other common platforms usually have free or inexpensive software programs called plugins that you can add to your website to enhance security.

Plugins like Wordfence, iThemes Security Pro and many others help minimize or slow down hackers that are trying to get into your site. I suggest that you speak with your webmaster about adding website security to your site ASAP.

10 Quick Reasons Why You May Need a New Site

1. Your site was built more than five years ago.
2. Your overall design is old and dated.
3. Your competitor's site looks much better than yours.
4. You always make excuses why your site looks so bad.
5. You're missing calls to action for the entire sales funnel.
6. You can't add content without going to your webmaster.
7. Your site has no blog or social media links.
8. Your site is NOT mobile-friendly.
9. Your site was built by a web or IT person that knows nothing about SEO or lead generation.
10. You have no way to convert visitors into leads that does not include, "Join my newsletter."

Website To-Do List

For New Sites.
- Find a company or person that knows as much about Internet marketing, SEO, and lead generation as they do about web design.
- Select a platform that you can easily add content to without a web master. A good choice is WordPress.
- Find the money to do it and get it done.

For Website Makeovers or Tweaks.
- Add some calls to action to cover every part of the sales funnel.
- Eliminate unnecessary pages.
- Eliminate "white noise" like flash images, music or videos that start automatically.
- Simplify navigation as much as possible.
- Update your site frequently with blogs, photos, and videos.

The Importance of "On-Site" SEO

If you're in the middle of a web design, or thinking about having someone redo your site, one major question to ask is if your web designer knows anything about lead generation or Search Engine Optimization (SEO). I speak often about the three different types of people and agencies that build and/or maintain websites:

1. **The 'Webmaster'** - Loves coding, flash, widgets, and the latest "stuff" on your site because it's cool.

2. **The 'Designer'** - What most people hire for. Great at making websites that look beautiful. These are graphics people and designers who don't necessarily care about code but thrive on making websites look stunning.

3. **The 'Marketer'** - The marketer's main concern? Can website visitors find what they're looking for? Does the site generate leads that eventually increase sales? In my biased opinion, this is the most important function of any website - be sure to consult with a website lead generation professional when updating a current site or creating a totally new website.

If you are hiring someone to do your website, don't just let the designer dictate things that have to do with generating leads. Remember, the designers work for you. Ultimately, it's your decision. Personally, I'd rather have a site that isn't as attractive but is on page one of Google than a beautiful site that's on page ten that will never be found.

Step 2

Use SEO To Get Your Website Lead Gen Ready

Creating an effective on-site SEO (search engine optimization) strategy is critical to the success of your business. But, before you get started, you need to know what specific keywords your prospects and customers are typing into the search engines to find your products and services. The next few pages will help you understand the different types of keywords (and there are many) and how and where to find them.

Keyword Fundamentals

When it comes to Internet marketing, the main role of keywords is to act as a bridge. Keywords help connect people and shoppers on search engines like Google and Bing with your website.

If you've optimized your website and your content, the chance that your business will appear high up in the search engine results, giving shoppers the opportunity to click increases dramatically.

I like to separate and classify keywords into two categories: *research keywords* and *buying keywords*. A good example is "*hot tubs*", which I consider to be a research keyword. Yet, "*hot tubs prices*", I consider to be a buying keyword. Both keyword types show different intent by the user.

The specific keyword or search term that a shopper or prospect types into a search engine gives you an indication of purchase intent - where they are in the customer journey, buying cycle or sales funnel.

A common keyword like *"hot tubs"* would normally be considered at the very top of the sales funnel. In most cases, interested buyers are still researching hot tubs in general. As you go further down the sales funnel, a keyword phrase like *"hot tub dealer"* has a different intent. At this stage, consumers may be looking for a local retailer.

Contrast that with a phrase like *"hot tub sale Dallas"*, which clearly shows purchase intent. This keyword phrase not only talks about intent to purchase, but also states a geographic area. An even stronger purchase intent keyword phrase might be something like *"price of a Hot Spring Aria in Dallas"*.

Long-tail Keywords

A long-tail keyword is a search term or a keyword phrase that is usually 3-7 words long. Generally, the volume for long-tail keywords, or the amount of people searching for this exact phrase is low, but the conversion is high.

Here's what SEMrush.com says about long-tail keywords...
Long-tail keyword phrases are keywords with low monthly search volume, but higher probability of conversion. And it's got a higher probability of conversion because it's generally more specific and much easier to understand, in terms of purchase intent or what someone is typing in, as opposed to trying to guess what someone is looking for when they're typing in the word.

So, it's typically lower search volume, but it's also lower competition and cheaper cost per click, CPC, as in compared to other word searches. In 2017, Google reported that nearly 15% of all searches were new and had never been searched before.

So, long-tail keywords typically have lower search volume, lower competition, and less cost per click (CPC) when compared to other word searches.

Long-tailed keywords are unique and change often to reflect public interest. In 2017, Google reported that nearly 15% of all searches were new and had never been searched before.
*https://www.semrush.com/kb/685-what-are-long-tailed-keywords

Why You Need to Move Beyond Your Basic Keywords.
In thinking through keywords, it makes sense to change our mindset a little bit. Remember, a solid keyword strategy involves far more than optimizing for a single keyword, like *"hot tubs"*.

Dealers often tell me, "We don't need to do any SEO because we already show on the first page of Google for "hot tubs." While this may be true, what about the hundreds of other long-tail keyword phrases your buyers are searching for? Especially the conversational keyword phrases that didn't exist a few years ago (think voice search).

Here's a simple test. Type *"hot tubs Chicago"* into Google and look at the results. When I did it, my search returned 35,500,000 results. This high number tells you something important: this specific keyword is a well searched phrase - and tough to try and rank on page one for.

Now, look at the search results from a few less popular, long-tail keywords:

Hot tub sales Chicago - 16 million
Hot tubs for sale in Chicago - 3.8 million
Used spas Chicago - 8.3 million
Hot tub dealer Chicago - 29.5 million

If you add up just a few of these "other than hot tubs" keywords you end up with more than the 35,500,000 search results for hot tubs. I'm not suggesting that you ignore *"hot tubs"*, just that you spend some time trying to rank for other, equally as important keywords.

Different Keywords Trigger Different Search Results.
In the same way the words we use in speech may have different meanings depending on how they're used, different keywords return different types of search results. Depending on the keyword intent, and Google's algorithm, you will see different results on the Search Engine Results Pages (SERP). Some keywords reflect purchase intent, while others are more informational.

Common Types of Search Engine Results:

- Google Shopping Ads
- Knowledge panel
- Organic website results
- Images
- Videos
- AdWords
- Google Maps
- Google My Business

If the goal is to rank for as many different types of results as possible, then you'll need to deploy different strategies for different keywords.

Overlooked & Mis-Used Keyword Strategies

Building a successful keyword strategy isn't complicated but does require that you master a few basics. While some would argue that it takes more art than science to perfect a keyword strategy, I've seen quite a few businesses succeed and a few make serious missteps. Here are some things to do, and others to avoid.

Use Social Media #Hashtags (Carefully).
Hashtags - the # symbol used before words on social media can be extremely valuable for building awareness, sparking conversation, and collating what's been said about an event, idea, or theme. But, used improperly, hashtags can derail even the best laid plans.

It's never a good idea to arbitrarily place a hashtag next to a keyword other than your own company name, unless you research the hashtag keyword first. For example, I typed #hottubs into Facebook and came up with a variety of articles, with titles like these:

- *How safe are hot tubs?* - Centers for Disease Control
- *Hot tub horror: Warning as villains stalk internet communities* (my personal favorite)
- *Staying healthy in a hot tub* – What is a hot tub? A stress free aqueous have or a water barrel brimming with bacteria?

Clearly, these are not the results you want potential buyers to stumble across after checking out a hashtag you've promoted. With that said, it's worth putting some time into researching a few hashtags - it's a fast and easy way to join the conversation and get a feel for what people are chatting about.

Consider Chatbot Keywords.
Automation can deliver great value when used in the right way. We used chatbots to implement a Facebook keyword strategy that works 24/7. First, we created a few strategic posts asking for input from followers. Then we asked them whether they wanted the next sales promotion to be on hot tubs or swim spas.

Once they typed in the targeted keyword (hot tubs or swim spas), we were able to send them an immediate response asking them if they'd like to receive advance notice of any upcoming sales. If they replied yes, then we received the green light to capture their contact information and follow up with them in the future.

Leverage Customer Reviews.
Another great way to use keywords is to encourage people to leave you a review on sites like Google, adding keywords, company names and locations. This is helpful because sometimes keywords help trigger reviews that show up in Google's Knowledge Panel, Google My Business or Google Maps. So, if someone types "*hot tubs city name*" into Google, it may return Google Maps and Google My Business results with a positive review of your business right there on the search result page including the keyword and city name!

Free Online Tools to Help You Do Keyword Research

There are a variety of free online tools to help you research the keywords you need to compete. Let's start with some of the free tools that Google provides:

Google Autocomplete.
If you haven't noticed before, as soon as you begin to type something into your Google search bar, Google provides suggestions in real time. This information is extremely valuable, as it shows you other popular searches related to what you are typing.

Here's another trick: if you type the keyword *"hot tubs"* into Google and then type the letter "A", it returns all the popular words that begin with "A" – like *"hot tubs Atlanta"*. Next, type *"hot tubs"* and "B" to get all the popular words that begin with "B" – like *"hot tubs Baltimore"*. It's possible to go through the entire alphabet gathering all the keywords that apply to you.

Google Related Searches.
After typing something into Google, take a close look at the results. At the very bottom of the page there's a section called "searches related to". Sometimes these words and phrases are related to and similar to the words in Google Autocomplete, but not always.

YouTube Autocomplete.
If you're trying to rank for a video, keywords generated by YouTube are not always the same as those returned from Google search. Consider using YouTube search to get some fresh ideas - extremely helpful if you're trying to improve how a video ranks.

Google Search Console. According to Google*

"Google Search Console is a free service offered by Google that helps you monitor, maintain, and troubleshoot your site's presence in Google Search results. You don't have to sign up for Search Console to be included in Google Search results, but Search Console helps you understand and improve how Google sees your site".

Search Console offers tools and reports for the following actions:
- Confirm that Google can find and crawl your site.
- Fix indexing problems and request re-indexing of new or updated content.
- View Google Search traffic data for your site: how often your site appears in Google Search, which search queries show your site, how often searchers click through for those queries, and more.
- Receive alerts when Google encounters indexing, spam, or other issues on your site.
- Show you which sites link to your website.
- Troubleshoot issues for AMP, mobile usability, and other Search features.

*https://support.google.com/webmasters/answer/9128668?hl=en

When you open your Google Search Console and click on "performance and queries", you will see the number of impressions and the number of clicks that have appeared over a certain period of time for specific keywords.

AdWords Keyword Planning Tool.
In order to use Google's AdWords Keyword Planning Tool, you must have an AdWords account. To find the keyword planner, open your AdWords account dashboard and click *"Tools"*, then click *"Keyword Planner"*.

Once inside the keyword planner, type in a targeted keyword and designate a specific geographic area. The planner will provide you with a list of related keywords, average monthly searches, competitive data, the top bid, and other relevant information.

Soovle.
If you visit soovle.com and type in a keyword, you will receive results from a variety of search engines and websites including Google, Wikipedia, Answers, YouTube, Bing, Yahoo, Amazon, e-Bay and a few more - a great way to cross reference your results.

Other free tools you may want to check out include: Keywordtool.io and KeywordsEverywhere.com

What is On-Site SEO?

On-site search engine optimization (SEO) are the things that you do on your site or to your site to make it easier for the search engines to find your business.

On-site SEO involves implementing a lot of little things that over time add up to something much bigger. It can involve optimizing your site for specific keywords, updating titles and descriptions to be sure that you are telling Google what every page on your website is about.

While onsite SEO is a critical part of developing your online presence for search engines like Google, you also want to be sure that you have informative content on the "front-end" of your website for visitors to consume.

SEO Fundamentals: Ranking, Optimizing & More

After all the research, brainstorming and developing you put into your SEO strategy, it can be maddening - and a bit confusing - as to why you're not ranking for important keywords. The simple answer is, you're probably targeting high volume short-tail keywords.

For example, say you're a local hot tub dealer that wants to rank for the keyword "*hot tubs*". This is what you're likely to see on Google's first page for a "*hot tub*" search: Amazon, Home Depot, Costco, Jacuzzi, etc. Despite your best efforts, you will rarely out rank (rank higher) than these well-established websites. And, many searches that come from these types of general keywords aren't even related to purchasing a hot tub at all, but generate from other topics like "*hotels with hot tubs*", "*hot tub time machine*", etc.

Just tell me what Google wants in terms of SEO and I'll give it to them!
Google's primary objective is to satisfy their users, so they keep using their search engine. Google wants essentially what every consumer wants when they visit your site: an easy, convenient resolution to a problem.
Online Searchers Want to:

- Find what they came looking for quickly and easily
- Get their questions answered fast
- Be educated about your company, products, and services
- Know if your company has what they need at a price they can afford
- Feel comfortable doing business with you

Does your website do all of this? If not, you need to get it done by someone who knows how to do it right. If you don't have the resources inside your company, consider hiring an outside consultant that understands your industry and knows what needs to be done to properly optimize your website.

The Importance of Mobile & Voice Search.
Consumers are radically changing the way they search for products and services online and voice-activated devices are playing a larger role. All these devices are essentially voice-activated virtual assistant chatbots. This means you need to optimize your on-site SEO to include popular voice search keywords.

But what are popular voice search keywords? One of the most common mobile search terms is *"near me."* For example, "*Where can I find a hot tub sale near me.*" With the popularity of voice enabled devices, it's critical you optimize your website and Google AdWords for terms like these.

Popular Mobile Search Terms:

- Near me, nearby, near [city] – *hot tub dealer near me, hot tub tale in San Diego*
- How do I… *how do I clean my spa filter?*

- Where can I find...*a hot tub sale near me?*
- Where is the closest...*hot tub dealer?*

What Are You Currently Telling Google About Your Business?
Google tries hard to understand and organize all the content included on your website – indexing is how they do it. While different pages are indexed at different times, your goal should be to have all your pages indexed. After all, the more Google knows about your site, the easier it is for them to add you to the search engine results page.

If you go to Google and type the word S-I-T-E, then a colon, and then your website address... (site: http://yourwebsiteaddress.com) the search results will show you how many pages Google has indexed related to your website.

This is also a quick way to see what you are telling Google about your business based on your website onsite SEO meta titles, descriptions, and keyword coding of your website.

If a page is indexed, Google must show something in their search results. If you don't tell them what your page is about, the search "bots" are forced to find something and publish it. Many times, it's the first sentence of each page but it could be just about anything on the page. Therefore, if you don't adjust your website's on-site SEO, Google will have no choice but to scrape random text from your site and put it on the search result.

What follows is a discussion on SEO fundamentals - tips and tricks to help you rank higher, optimize better, and get more out of your SEO strategy.

15 Tips & Tricks to Rank Higher

1. Optimize Meta Header Tags.
A simple "under the hood" task that can help Google understand your webpages better is adjusting your Header tags. Header tags are classified by H1, H2, H3 or Heading 1, Heading 2 or Heading 3.

H1 tags are usually the most important text on a page and most often the title of the page. If you have a WordPress site, there is a setting on every page where you can adjust the header tags. <h1> Important Text</h1>.

Many times, built-in coding automatically makes the page name or blog post title an H1 tag, but it depends on your website software. Whenever possible, I suggest you add targeted keywords and towns in your H1 tags. <h1>Hot Tubs Chicago</h1>

2. Optimize Meta Titles & Descriptions.
Page meta titles and descriptions are what your customers <u>and</u> prospects actually see in the search engine results from Google, Bing, Yahoo, and other search engines when they type in specific keyword phrases.

A strategically written meta page title of approximately 60 characters and meta page description between 140-160 characters can significantly improve your chances of showing up higher in the search results. Just be sure that you write for both the search engines and consumers. In other words, write naturally, as you would speak and avoid "keyword stuffing" in an effort to rank higher with Google – it won't work.

3. Be Strategic with Keyword Placement & LSI Keywords.
If possible and appropriate, it's always a good idea to place your targeted keywords in the first sentence of the first and last paragraph of each page. In addition to adding your most important keywords, you should also add LSI keywords (Latent Semantic Indexing).

LSI Keywords are additional keywords that are related to the main keyword that your customers or prospects search for on search engines like Google. Think of them as synonyms. If you scroll down to the bottom of the page for any Google search, you'll normally see a section called "related searches" which normally contain similar LSI keywords.

An example of this would be the main keyword of *"hot tubs"* and an LSI or related search term of *"portable spas."* Including strategically placed keywords and LSI keywords helps optimize your pages, increasing your site's chances of ranking higher in the search engine results.

4. Link Related Pages to One Another Using Anchor Text.
One way to help Google quickly understand the structure of your website is to link related pages to each other using on page "anchor text".

Internal links can appear on any page and point the reader to another page on the website related to a word or topic being discussed. This is done by hyperlinking a specific word (anchor text). Here's an example. Soaking in a hot tub is a great form of ***hydrotherapy***. In this case, I could link the word hydrotherapy (a related word to hot tubs) to a blog you may have written on your website.

By adding anchor text keyword links throughout your website, you connect readers to relevant and related topics that they may want to read more about. In addition, linking related pages helps Google understand the relevance of those pages, adding value to linked pages – all of which can help improve website optimization. Here is the code to use when linking pages using the example above:
<a href=" https://en.wikipedia.org/wiki/Hydrotherapy/" title="hydrotherapy">hydrotherapy</a>

5. Add Social Media Sharing Buttons to Improve Social Signals.
Adding social sharing buttons is a subtle yet highly effective on-page optimization technique. It gives your website visitors the ability to share your site's content with just one click, driving more traffic to your website.

Referrals, likes, shares and backlinks from social media sites like Facebook and Twitter provide search engines like Google "social signals" and is supposedly helpful as one of the many aspects of their ranking algorithms.

6. Optimize Page Names (Permalinks) Whenever Possible.
Creating simple and SEO friendly page names or 'permalinks' gives each page a little more search engine targeted relevance. A permalink is the text that comes after the back slash on any URL. For example, **www.WebsiteName/This-Is-The-Permalink**. Just make sure that your permalink isn't too long.

And, rather than **www.WebsiteName.com/Contact-Us**, use targeted keywords and town combinations – **www.WebsiteName.com/Hot-Tub-Dealer-Chicago**.

It can be tricky to go back in and do this for established websites because of all the internal links and all the places the older page might already be indexed around the Internet. However, creating optimized permalinks for new pages and blog posts is easy and highly recommended.

7. Don't Miss the Opportunity for 'On Page' Text.
Google crawls and indexes website pages by "reading" text. So, you it's not a smart idea to have only photos on your pages. Even if images have text on them, it doesn't matter, because Google can't read the text on photos.

As just mentioned in the Meta Tag section, if Google doesn't have enough text to create a description of a page, it will search and insert whatever text it finds. Most likely, this will not accurately describe what is on that specific page. Therefore, it is best practice to have at least 500 to 1000 words of text on all your important pages.

8. Check Your Website Speed.
A fast-loading site, or a fast-loading page, is critical. Google, and all your website visitors will not appreciate slow loading pages.

Think of your own experience - how many times have you typed something into Google, clicked on a link and gone to the site only to be stuck in a "loading" pattern. Frustrated, you hit the back button, return to Google, and select the next choice on the list.

Website visitors are always one "back click button" away from leaving your site and therefore will usually not wait around very long for your slow website to load. This increases your website "bounce rate" and kills your lead conversion rate.

A Slow Loading Site Can Occur for a Variety of Reasons Including:
- An old site built more that 5-7 years ago using old, outdated code
- Too much flash or complicated and unnecessary html code
- Uploading and showing videos directly from your website rather than embedding YouTube videos
- Slow loading graphics – which is a very common occurrence

One way to check your website speed is to take a speed test. There is a site called **pingdom.com** where you can type in a URL, and it will give you a speed performance grade.

However, don't get too hung up on a performance grade. Just understand that the faster you can get your site to load, and get people where they want to go, the better it is for you and your website visitors.

9. Improve Site Speed with Image Optimization.
As you might imagine, many dealers either take great photos themselves or use the professional photos provided by their vendors and upload them to the appropriate pages on their website.

Unfortunately, most of the time dealers upload high-resolution images (hi-res) which can slow down the load time speed of the website. If you're going to upload photos to your site, (which I encourage you to do) be sure that they are low-res versions.

With a printed brochure, you want to be sure to use high-resolution 300 dpi (dots per inch) photos. But on a website, you don't need print quality, high-resolution photos. All you really need for web viewing are low-resolution 72 dpi photos – they look good and load much faster.

You may be adding stunning, even low-resolution graphics to your site about a current sale or a new product, but many times, that content including all the specs or promo details are only contained within the image with no other descriptive written text. As mentioned previously, Google can't read text on photos and you're not getting the benefit of that text content.

In addition, since the content showed up as an image, those words aren't getting indexed. Now, Google can't tell a customer that's shopping that you're having a sale that weekend.

The way to fix this is by using ALT image tags. This is code associated with each photo that tells Google what the photo is about. There is code made available for the ALT image tag when you upload a photo.

When you hover over it, you're going to see the ALT image tag show up telling you a variety of different things about the photo. Here is the code I use, but I suggest you ask your webmaster to implement this strategy using the code they prefer.

10. Use You Tube When Uploading Videos.
Many dealers create great videos and upload them to their site. Then, when a visitor clicks, the video plays directly from the website. The problem is, when you upload video directly to your site, it requires a great deal of storage space and a lot of bandwidth to view, which slows down your site.

I recommend uploading videos to your YouTube channel first, and then embedding them into your site. This way, the video is hosted someplace else and does not slow down your site. Plus, you get twice the exposure: first, with YouTube, which can be picked up by other search engines or other resources, and second, on your own site.

11. Make Sure Your NAP Matches Google.

It is important that make sure that the business name, address and phone number or NAP on your website matches the NAP on your Google My Business (GMB) page. This helps Google accurately identify you as the owner of the GMB page. And, be exact. If your GMB listing says 123 Main St and your website says 123 Main Street, that is NOT a match. I suggest that you change your website to match the GMB listing versus the reverse whenever possible.

12. Create a Site Map.

A site map is essentially a listing of all the pages that you have on your website. Few consumers take advantage of the sitemap, but Google certainly does.

Adding a site map helps Google index more of your pages when they send bots or spiders to "scan" your site. The more pages that are indexed, the more likely your products and services will get found by customers and prospects.

13. Decrease Your Bounce Rate.

According to Google… "A bounce is a single-page session on your site. In Analytics, a bounce is calculated specifically as a session that triggers only a single request to the Analytics server, such as when a user opens a single page on your site and then exits without triggering any other requests to the Analytics server during that session." *

Basically, visitors' bounce when they don't find what they need, and move on from your site. Paying close attention to how and where your visitors bounce can help you understand where you can improve.

"*Bounce rate is single-page sessions divided by all sessions, or the percentage of all sessions on your site where users viewed only a single page and triggered only a single request to the Analytics server."

*https://support.google.com/analytics/answer/1009409?hl=en

Quick Ways to Decrease Your Bounce Rate and Improve Time Spent on Your Site:

- Serve up better content
- Prompt visitors to use your navigation
- Create faster load time
- Improve website layout design
- Make your site mobile-friendly
- Optimize on-site SEO

14. Link to Your 'Google My Business' Page.
Adding a link on your *Location* or *Contact Us* page to your Google My Business (GMB) page provides a little boost because it helps Google show the connection between the two sites.

15. Consider SEO Plugins.
There are many WordPress plugins available to help you optimize your website. Two of the most popular are listed below along with a description of each found on Wordpress.org.

I've used both plugins successfully, but suggest you speak with your website developer for more information and to get their input.

All in One SEO (https://wordpress.org/plugins/all-in-one-seo-pack/)
Use All in One SEO Pack to optimize your WordPress site for SEO. It's easy and works out of the box for beginners and has advanced features and an API for developers.

Yoast (https://wordpress.org/plugins/wordpress-seo/)
Since 2008, Yoast SEO has helped millions of websites worldwide to rank higher in search engines. This WordPress SEO plugin helps you with your search engine optimization. Are you not entirely convinced? Yoast SEO is the favorite WordPress SEO plugin of millions of users worldwide! As Yoast's mission is SEO for everyone, the plugin's users range from the bakery around the corner to some of the most popular sites on the planet.

Schema Markup

Search engines are constantly expanding the tools available to website owners and SEO specialists in order to create more value for users and help them find what the information they seek. One of the newest and most under-utilized SEO tools is website Schema markup. Here's a crash course on what it is and how you can benefit from it.

I know some of the information in this section may get a little "geeky" but hang in there as the end result of using schema markup is well worth it and besides, you can just hire someone (like us) to implement a schema strategy for you.

What is Schema Markup?
Schema is specific coding developed by search giants Google, Yahoo, Microsoft, and Yandex to create a unified structured data standard for all websites to use, that will be recognized by all search engines.

The Schema markup code essentially tells the search engines more specifically what a specific website page is about, beyond just what your meta tags and content says. By leveraging schema markup on your website, you can increase your chances of ranking well with search engines so that more potential customers find your business.

Basically, the structured data in the Schema markup works as a system of pairing a name with a value that helps search engines categorize and index your content

Some of the information in this section may get a little "geeky," but hang in there as the end result of using schema markup is well worth it.

Google describes the data this way…

"Google Search works hard to understand the content of a page. You can help us by providing explicit clues about the meaning of a page to Google by including structured data on the page.

Structured data is a standardized format for providing information about a page and classifying the page content; for example, on a recipe page, what are the ingredients, the cooking time and temperature, the calories, and so on."

*https://developers.google.com/search/docs/guides/intro-structured-data

What are the Best Types of Schema for a Local Business?
Let's look at a few ways you can quickly improve your website using schema markup.

Local Business
The Schema local business markup displays essential and relevant information about the location of a business or a local branch of an organization. It also helps customers to easily find the company's location and other information, featuring the address, opening hours, contact information as well as related social media links.

You want to give Google, Yahoo, and Bing everything they need to share with potential customers who might be searching for your products or services. For example, if search engine bots can't locate your address or hours on your website, they can't return that information in their search results. The more relevant information you provide search engines, the better.

Q&A (Frequently Asked Questions)
FAQ pages are a good place for schema, because these pages are frequented by first-time visitors looking to educate themselves about your business and its policies. Q&A and FAQ sections can help identify the best and most popular answers, helping people get the answers they need much faster.

One of the newer tools in Schema, these tags define webpages that are focused on raising questions and answering them. Traditionally very useful for FAQ pages, these tags make it easy for users to read questions and answers from your site.

Which Pages Should You Consider Adding Schema to?
Now that you know what the Schema markup is all about and saw the most common types of markups out there, it's time to see which pages you should consider adding Schema to for your business. Here are three to get you started.

Location Pages.
This is part of local SEO. People need to know that they're finding the site for a local business and not a business of the same name somewhere on the other end of the country.

Products and Services You Offer.
Using schema markup for the products or services you offer gives you a better chance of being noticed by potential customers.

FAQ (Frequently Asked Questions).
While Google can still usually identify an FAQ page without markup, as I mentioned earlier, it is still a good idea to Schema here.

Can Schema Improve SEO, If So, How?
By leveraging schema, you're making it easier for search engines to find your site and share it with the most relevant end users. While there are hundreds of SEO tips and tricks that claim to enhance your overall search engine rankings, taking the time to invest in schema can only improve your chances of SEO success. Many studies point to improved click-through rates, more time spent on pages, and greater customer engagement.

Ultimately, the easier you make it for search engines to deliver relevant information and the more trust you build online, the higher you will rank on the search engines over time.

Step 3

Drive Traffic

These days, too many dealers engage in what I call "stop and go" marketing: sales come in, so they STOP marketing. Then, sales slow down, so they START marketing. Sales come in again, so they STOP marketing. The cycle repeats, again and again.

This is a dangerous form of marketing because your marketing costs invariably get larger and your sales increases become smaller. The better approach to take is to have an ongoing and consistent Internet marketing strategy. Remember, your current level of organic traffic is <u>not</u> guaranteed, and your competition is getting smarter. So, investing in Internet marketing is investing in your future!

There are 3 main goals of any successful Internet marketing strategy. You want to:

1. Be where your prospects are searching
2. Position your business better than your competition
3. Provide Google with recent and relevant content

Now let's look at the two main ways of driving traffic to your website – paid ads or organic marketing.

Pay-Per-Click Advertising vs. Organic SEO Marketing

With tons of information available online, it's getting harder and harder to rank on page #1 of Google. In addition to constant algorithm changes at Google, you're also competing with:

- Hot Tub, Pool and Sauna Factories
- Paid Shopping Results
- Pay-Per-Click – AdWords
- Online Directories and Yellow Pages
- Review Sites – Angi, Yelp
- Other pool, spa, and sauna dealers

But why do you "deserve" to be on page #1? It's not because you have the lowest prices or sell the highest quality products. Or, because you offer the best service or have been in business for 20 years. High organic ranking businesses "earn" the right to be on page one because they provide the search engines quality content that is recent and relevant to the people searching for specific keyword search terms. Sound easy? Here's a breakdown of strategies, along with the pros and cons of each to get you started.

You've probably heard about pay-per-click advertising and organic search marketing, but which is better? The short answer to both can work well, it just depends on how and what you measure.

Here's a quick breakdown of the pros and cons, with more detail on each below.

Pay-Per-Click Advertising (PPC)

Pros.
- Results can be almost immediate
- Turn it on and off at will
- Can quickly outrank competitors
- Great place to test things fast

Cons.
- Can waste a lot of money quickly if not done right
- No residual value
- Once you stop paying Google, your online marketing disappears
- Can detract from organic results – they click on your ad vs your organic results on the same page

Organic SEO
Pros.
- Results can last for years
- Since 75+/-% of clicks come from organic, initial investment eventually turns into "free" clicks
- Dozens of strategies to choose from
- Improves your website ranking
- Good content marketing can improve your "authority & brand"
- Some people just don't click on ads

Cons.
- Results take longer to appear
- Requires a more organized and coordinated effort

How does AdWords stack up against posting on Facebook? Organic marketing like Facebook can fill the top of your sales funnel for the future, while pay-per-click strategies, like AdWords do a good job at attracting "low hanging fruit" where competitors spend most of their time and money. Engaging prospects early in the buying cycle is key! In my opinion, this is better achieved through organic marketing.

With AdWords marketing, people are intentionally searching for specific keywords, and you bid for those keywords. This is different from organic Facebook marketing, where people are connecting with friends, and not looking for products and services. In this case, you bid not on specific keywords, but for potential buyers based on your demographic and psychographic target market.

Paid Traffic (PPC): Google AdWords

If you've decided to give paid traffic a try, Google AdWords is a great place to start. But there are three critical things you need to do before getting started.

1. Implement Best Practices When Setting Up Campaigns.
First, before you do anything else, you need to create a single G-mail account for all your Google properties – Google Analytics, Search Console, Google My Business and YouTube. Doing this provides AdWords with much more information that can be used to optimize your AdWords campaigns, improve click through rates and increase conversions.

Next, implement the following AdWords best practices:

Add a Privacy Policy to Your Website.
Google looks to see if you have a privacy policy when they evaluate your keyword quality scores. A higher quality score for specific keywords can lower your cost per click.

Add Measurable "Calls to Action" on Your Website and Keep Them Visible on Every Page.
One of the ways that you measure the effectiveness of AdWords is by conversions. And, you can't have a conversion unless you have a call to action that suggests or leads a prospect down a specific sales funnel.

Align Calls to Action with the Customer Journey.
Different types of calls to action need to be created for different parts of the sales journey. Why? People at the top of the funnel may not know what 'ozone' is or the value of using a salt-water system. Advertising that targets ozone or a free saltwater system will likely only appeal to prospects who have done the research and know what these items are and how much they are worth.

On the other hand, someone that just sat in a hot tub for the first-time last night and does a search for "hot tubs Chicago" on Google is probably looking for basic information, and not likely to be a buyer at this point in the sales journey.

2. Automate & Systemize Your Follow-Up.
Without downplaying the importance of human interaction, you want a system in place that works 24/7, whether you're working or not.

Quite a few leads come after normal business hours, and you probably don't want to have to answer the phone or send an e-mail at that time. With an automated, systemized approach to generating and following up with leads in place, you won't have to.

Your lead generation system needs to automatically deliver whatever you promised. So, if you're offering a hot tub buyer's guide, it needs to be delivered immediately. A thank you email should be sent to prospects immediately, followed by a notification email to your sales team letting them know that a lead was recently generated.

3. Create a Unique Landing Page.
Never send AdWords traffic to your website homepage. You may sell several different types of products, all prominently featured on your homepage.

But you may only be using AdWords to advertise hot tubs. Why make a visitor who clicks on a hot tub ad work harder than they need to by forcing them to sift through your homepage to find the right hot tub link?

Instead, create a unique landing page for each product line you target with AdWords. Your landing page should not be accessible to the general public, and therefore should not appear anywhere in your website's navigation. This makes it much easier to track AdWords analytics.

What to Include on an AdWords Landing Page.
Creating a high-performing AdWords landing page isn't complicated, you just need to know what to include.

Headlines.
First, create a compelling headline that matches your ad. Write something that grabs the reader's attention, like *"Hot Tub Clearance Sale"*. Next, create a sub-headline that invites them to continue reading down the page.

Photos & Video.
> Include a photo of your offer and a few lines of copy that describes the offer in more detail. If you're offering *0% financing for 48 months* – it should be there. Also, don't forget that whatever was promised in the ad needs to be on the landing page - these are the details of your deal like pricing, financing, freebies, etc.

At Least a Little Copy.
> Your landing page needs decent graphics, videos, and at least some text. Avoid having just a picture and nothing else. While people can read it, Google can't, and it doesn't help your quality score if you don't have some text on the page.

Social Proof.
> Finally, it's helpful to include social proof, or even better, a rating from the Better Business Bureau (BBB). In fact, credibility-building elements like these aren't just for the landing page but should be everywhere on your site.

Structure & Targeting Options.
At the very highest level, AdWords consists of campaigns, with specific ad groups beneath. I suggest that you separate ad groups by product types – hot tubs, swim spas, saunas, etc. Under each ad group are unique ads and under each ad are keywords associated with those ads.

When you first set up an AdWords campaign, there are several different options you can choose, such as *search network* and *display*. If you're doing this for the first time, Google will prompt you to select one.

Here are a few of the other options for targeting.

Locations
> Be sure that if you're in Chicago, you're not advertising in Boston. When you set up your campaigns, Google gives you several different options in the location settings section.

Radius Targeting

If you created a 20-mile radius around Chicago, this will graphically show you what that radius includes. And, you can zoom in or out to make sure your radius includes the areas that you want.

City Targeting

By inputting Chicago for example, it will list the city and graphically show you what area it includes.

Zip Code Targeting

You can also type in zip codes and advertise just to people within those areas.

Developing a Keyword Strategy that Gets Results

Now that you're more familiar with what AdWords is and how it works, let's look at the different kinds of keyword search types, how they're used and where to find them. *

Google Describes Keyword Types This Way*:

Broad Match.

Broad match is the default match type that all your keywords are assigned. Ads may show on searches that include misspellings, synonyms, related searches, and other relevant variations. So, if your keyword is "women's hats," someone searching for "buy ladies hats" as well as "women's scarves" might see your ad.

Broad Match Modifier.

Broad match modifiers are similar to broad match, except that the broad match modifier option only shows ads in searches that include the words with a plus sign "+" in front of them (+women's hats), or close variations of the "+" terms.

Phrase Match.
> Ads may show on searches that match a phrase, or close variations of that phrase, which may include additional words before or after.

> Ads won't show, however, if a word is added to the middle of the phrase that changes the meaning of the phrase. Phrase match is designated with quotation marks ("women's hats").

Exact Match.
> Ads may show on searches that match the exact term or are close variations of that exact term. Close variants include searches for keywords with the same meaning as the exact keywords, regardless of spelling or grammar differences between the query and the keyword. Exact match is designated with brackets ([red shoe]).

* https://support.google.com/google-ads/answer/7478529?hl=en

**Keywords vs. Search Terms. **
According to Google, a "KEYWORD" is the word or set of words that Google advertisers create for a given ad group to target your ads to customers.

A "SEARCH TERM" is the exact word or set of words a customer enters when searching on Google.com or one of our Search Network sites.

Use the search terms report to identify new search terms with high potential and add them to your keyword list. When building your list, look for search terms that aren't as relevant to your business, and add them as negative keywords. This can help you avoid spending money showing your ad to people who aren't interested in it.

**https://support.google.com/google-ads/answer/2472708?hl=en

"Research" vs. "Buying" Keywords. (for more detailed info, see previous section on keywords)
Over the years, I have developed my own strategy for classifying keywords. I believe that the phrase *"hot tubs"* is a research keyword as opposed to the phrase *"hot tub prices"*, which is a buying keyword phrase.

Someone who types *"hot tubs San Antonio"* might be a good prospect for a hot tub buyer's guide because they may still be in the research phase of buying a hot tub. Compare that with someone who types in *"hot tub prices San Antonio"*, who might have already done the research, and might be more interested in getting a hot tub price quote.

It's helpful to create separate ad groups based on buyer intent – 'buying' keywords like *"hot tub sale"* or *"hot tub price"* for example and "research" keywords like *"hot tubs"* and *"hot tub dealer."* I also recommend that you create an ad group specifically for local competitors.

Where to Find All These Important Keywords.
By clicking on the *tools* tab in Google AdWords, you'll find their keyword planner tool. Type in a specific keyword and the tool will provide you with many different keyword suggestions that are relevant or related to your original keyword. It also gives you the average monthly searches for that specific keyword.

AdWords Settings That Most People Miss

AdWords is designed to make it as easy as possible to build your online business through targeted leads. But that doesn't mean businesses don't make mistakes. Here are a few settings that more than a few people miss when setting up an AdWords campaign.

Negative Keywords.
Be sure that you don't pay for clicks that you don't want, words like sex, hotel, rental, movie etc. Remember the movie "Hot Tub Time Machine"? You don't want to pay for those clicks!

Dealers actually ended up paying for those clicks! I don't know why someone would type in *"hot tub time machine"*, and click on a hot tub dealer ad, but they do, and you just paid for that.

If you're not offering hot tub rentals, you don't want to pay for an ad that says, "*Hot tub rentals Chicago*". Avoid this by putting the word "rental" in the negative keywords section of AdWords.

From the keywords section, click on the plus button and add any negative keywords. Now, if someone types in *"sex in a hot tub"*, you won't get a click for that and your ads won't show for that phrase or others you don't want, like *"hotels with hot tubs"* etc.

Time of Day.
AdWords will also let you adjust your ads to show or not show on specific days or time of day. I have a B2B (business to business) AdWords client whose customers don't work on weekends. So, we shut ads off completely on Saturdays and Sundays.

Device Bid Adjustments.
Review your AdWords stats to see which devices are sending you the most clicks and conversions. You may be surprised to learn that mobile devices (phones and tablets) send you the majority of clicks. If this is the case, it may be worth paying a premium to have your ads show up higher on mobile devices.

In campaign settings, you can make a "device bid adjustment", bidding more for mobile devices with full browsers, computers, and tablets. Basically, you tell Google that whatever your normal bid is for each keyword, you're willing to pay just a little bit more to have your ad show up higher in mobile. I usually add a 10% premium for mobile devices.

Click-to-Call.
When your ads show up on a mobile device like a cell phone, a small phone icon shows on the screen. With this feature enabled, consumers can simply click on the icon, and it will call automatically, dialing whatever number you provide to Google.

You can tell Google which number to call in one of two ways. One, it can be tied directly to your Google My Business (GMB) location. Or two, you can provide a specific phone number via a phone site link.

It's also possible to use one of Google's phone numbers. By doing this, you'll be able to see how many people (visible in your conversion metrics) clicked on the ad that had a Google number enabled, and how many people called.

AdWords Measuring, Testing & Improving

Now that you've entered your targeted keywords and your ads are running, you'll want to know how effective your campaigns are. Are they successful? There are many ways to measure success, so let's discuss split testing, conversions, CTR (click-through rate) and quality score.

Split Testing.
You always want to run more than one ad at one time. This is called "split testing" and is like a controlled science experiment. The purpose of split testing is that you can make slight changes to your ads over time, comparing as you go to see if those changes create better results. Caution: if you make too many changes at once, you'll never know which specific word changes improved the results.

With multiple ads running, you can go to the campaign dashboard and compare how many impressions, clicks and conversions each ad received.

So, when measuring ad effectiveness, what should you be looking at? Number of clicks? Click through rate, conversions, conversion rate? The answer is a sarcastic "yes." You need to look at all these stats, using the information provided to decide which ads you need to change or continue to run unchanged.

Although the metrics you receive provide important information, many of the decisions you make concerning ad changes are as much art as they are science.

Conversions.
Under the 'tools tab', you'll see 'conversions'. This is where you can set up all your conversion parameters. A conversion is simply some action that website visitors take that you want to measure. This could be requesting a price quote, filling out a form, or even calling you by phone.

Follow the prompts carefully when setting up each conversion. When you're finished, you will be provided with a conversion code that you'll need to add to the conversion page on your website.

Conversion pages are normally thank-you pages that website visitors are taken to after "opting-in" for something. Whenever someone lands on that particular page from an AdWords ad, Google will count that as a conversion. You also have the option of importing goals you set up on Google Analytics and use them as conversions. Ask your AdWords expert which one is best for you.

Keyword Quality Score.
Quality score relates specifically to the keywords that you're targeting. The quality score is an automated measurement that Google applies after comparing your ad to your AdWords landing page to see if the ad matches the content of landing page. In other words, keyword quality score determines how relevant the landing page is to the ad and if it successfully reflects what the website visitor was originally searching for.

Keyword quality score is determined by how well it meets the expectations of the person that clicked on the ad. The higher the quality score, the more it meets that expectation. Low quality scores often mean that the content on your landing page does not match the keyword typed in or the ad. Unfortunately, you will probably be charged more on a per click basis for a low-quality score. Therefore, be sure that whatever you say on your landing page matches the ad.

Common AdWords Mistakes That Cost You Money

AdWords should NOT be turned on to "set it and forget it" mode. Unfortunately, even if you're getting traffic, you can't just turn it on and walk away. Why? You will get traffic, but it will be very expensive traffic. Here are 4 common mistakes that you want to avoid.

Relying on AdWords Express (Now Called Smart Campaigns). Google offers a service called *AdWords Express* that automatically manages all the important AdWords settings. I personally don't like AdWords Express. I think it's more expensive, and your options are limited compared to normal AdWords. Yes, it's easier, but you'll pay for it. And to me, it's less effective.

Using Industry Lingo in You Ad. Many vendors create quarterly promotions tied to a specific product line, product innovation or trademarked name. It's a great way for the factory to communicate to their dealer base.

But many of these terms are meaningless and unknown to a first-time buyer. Rather than use industry lingo, use language that all people understand, not just hot tub enthusiasts. For example, instead of advertising "Crystal Clear Hot Tub Sale", advertise "Salt-Water Hot Tub Sale".

Failing to Monitor the Metrics. You should review your AdWords stats every month. Failing to do so can cost you time and energy in rewriting ads and deprive you of important details on ad performance.

Not Updating Your Website Specials Page. Always be sure that you update your specials page or any other page you use as a landing page for your ads. Having outdated information on these pages will negatively affect your keyword quality score and may also upset and confuse your customers and prospects.

Organic Traffic: Facebook Marketing

I'm not going to spend a lot of time discussing the merits of using Facebook for standard "organic" daily posting. Why? According to a recent study, the average organic reach for Facebook is only 6.4%*

* https://wearesocial.com/blog/2018/07/internet-growth-accelerates-but-facebook-ad-engagement-tumbles

This means that for the time and resources you spend on daily non-paid posting, as few as 6.4% of your friends, fans and followers actually see those posts. Organic reach has been declining for years. In fact, many people speculate that Facebook did this intentionally to encourage businesses to spend money on advertising. I tend to agree.

So, if you want to use Facebook to engage with your audience, you're going to have to budget for it. Although Facebook engagement can be useful in promoting your brand, I'm more interested in generating leads versus getting more "likes." And this brings us to a discussion on Facebook advertising.

Facebook Advertising: The Basics

When it comes to buying a hot tub, pool, swim spa, sauna, etc., the basic difference between Facebook advertising and Google AdWords is simple. When people use Google, they intentionally type in specific keywords searching for information, products, and services. When people use Facebook, they're primarily looking to connect with friends and entertain themselves with information they find interesting and amusing online. Rarely are Facebook users actively searching for products and services.

The motivations behind why people use search engines are intent based. In other words, people use search engines like Google and Bing because they want to find something, i.e., specific information, products, and services. And they type in specific keywords to find what they are looking for. Knowing this, savvy advertisers bid for these same keywords to try and make sure that their ads show up during a prospective buyer's search.

Facebook advertising is what has been referred to as more "interruption-based" advertising. Essentially, this means that your ad "interrupts" the original reason people use Facebook in the first place - to connect with friends and family. For ads to be effective, they must be relevant to the user and really stand out.

Based on my comments above, I will not review any organic Facebook posting strategies. Instead, I will focus on the various types of Facebook advertising that I have used effectively for years.

My definition of an 'effective Facebook ad' is one that drives traffic to your website and generates leads containing contact information - names, email addresses, phones, zip codes, etc. Said another way, I am more interested in leads versus "likes".

Facebook Marketing Objectives.
Below are the 3 different types of marketing objectives that Facebook currently offers along with the short description that Facebook provides for each:

1. Awareness
- Brand Awareness - Increase awareness for your brand by reaching people who are more likely to be interested in it.
- Reach - Show your ad to the maximum number of people

2. Consideration
- Traffic - Show your ad to the maximum number of people
- Engagement - Get more post engagements, Page likes, event responses or offer claims
- App installs - Get more people to install your app.
- Video views - Get more people to view your video
- Lead generation - Drive more sales leads from people interested in your brand or business.
- Messages - Get more people to send messages to your business in Messenger or WhatsApp.

3. Conversion
- Conversions - Drive valuable actions on your website, app or in Messenger.
- Catalog sales - Create ads that automatically show items from your catalog based on your target audience.
- Store traffic - Create ads that automatically show items from your catalog based on your target audience.

I like to focus my efforts on only 3 of the listed campaign objectives: *Traffic*, used for Facebook retargeting; *Lead generation* and *Conversions*, used for lead ads.

Other Facebook Marketing Options.
In addition to defining your marketing objective, Facebook allows you to choose from a variety of additional options.

Audience
This option allows you to create a new custom audience and define who you want to see your ads for hot tubs based on 3 criteria:

Geography/Locations; *Age* and *Gender*. I normally select ages 35 – 65+, choose both male and female and a specific radius around each store – i.e., 25 miles.

Detailed Targeting
Detailed targeting lets you select specific demographics, interests, or behaviors. In recent years, Facebook removed several demographic options like 'homeowners', forcing business owners to try and appeal to prospects through specific interests. I often use 'home and garden', 'home improvement', 'luxury items', 'travel', 'swimming' and other interests that fit the profile of someone who might be interested in hot tubs, swim spas and saunas.

Ad Placements
- Facebook news feed
- Instagram feed
- Facebook marketplace
- Instagram explore

Stories
- Facebook stories
- Instagram stories
- Messenger stories

In-Stream
- Facebook in-stream videos

If you choose the default/automatic Facebook ad placements, your ads will be shown on both Facebook and Instagram. I normally click on "edit placement," and remove Instagram as I don't think this platform is a good target market for high priced products like in ground pools, hot tubs, and swim spas. There may be more value in the future if the age of Instagram users continues to increase. But for now, I wouldn't recommend placing ads there.

Audience Size
The accuracy of estimates is based on factors like past campaign data, the budget you entered and market data. Numbers are provided to give you an idea of performance for your budget but are only estimates and don't guarantee results.

The more you adjust placements, demographics, and radius size, the more your audience will shrink or expand. Therefore, adjust only until you find a good size audience.

Budget and Schedule
Define how much you'd like to spend daily for your entire campaign. I normally select the "run my ad continuously" option and base my ad spend on the number of link clicks versus impressions. I don't like impressions because I prefer to pay for performance.

Building a Facebook Ad.
Once you have selected all your settings, it's time to create your Facebook ad. Again, there are multiple options available to help you create a customized ad that meets your needs as described by Facebook.

Format
Define the structure of your ad: single image or video or carousel.

Media
Choose an image or video or create a new video or slideshow using a template.

Primary Text
Three lines of primary text will show on Facebook Mobile News Feed before the link to view more.

Headline
The headline will appear in most placements, but its position will vary by placement. Headlines over 40 characters may be cut off.

Description
The description is additional text that appears in some placements. Its position on the ad varies by placement.

Display link
This option shows a shortened link instead of your full website URL in some placements. The link should go to the same domain as your website URL. The position of the display link varies by placement.

Call to Action
Allows you to show a button or link on your ad that represents the action you want people to take. Common calls to action:

- Apply Now
- Book Now
- Download
- Get Offer
- Get Quote
- Learn More
- Sign Up
- Subscribe

Conversion Tracking with a Facebook Pixel
Add pixel code to your website to track conversions, see activity and build audiences for ad targeting.

Installed, your Facebook pixel on your website gives you access to important traffic and conversion stats that you can use to determine the effectiveness of your ads. Use data captured by your Facebook pixel to reach people who took specific actions such as adding to cart.

Create Audience
There are 2 different types of custom audiences as outlined by Facebook:

- <u>Custom Audience via Upload</u>: A Custom Audience from a list is a type of audience you can create made up of your existing contacts. You can target ads to the audience you've created on Facebook, Instagram, and Audience Network. Basically, you upload, copy, and paste or import your hashed list, then we use the hashed data from it to match the people on your list to people on Facebook. (Note: Facebook doesn't learn any new identifying information about you.)

- <u>Create an Audience of Your Website Visitors</u>: This is where you can upload either phone numbers or emails and Facebook will take those emails and compare that to the emails that Facebook users use to log on. And if it matches, then you can actually advertise just to those people. I've uploaded 5,000 emails from dealer prospects and usually get between 40 and 60% of them to "stick".

Creating a customized audience like this allows you to do Facebook *retargeting*. Facebook retargeting works the same way that Google retargeting works. Basically, when a visitor to your website leaves and logs into Facebook, they can see your ad. Once they see that ad and click on that ad, it's up to you to send them to a specific landing page with a specific offer.

More information about custom audiences can be found here –

*https://www.facebook.com/business/help/341425252616329?id=24
69097953376494

Look-a-like Audience *
A Look-a-like Audience gives you a way to reach new people who
are likely to be interested in your business because they're similar to
your best existing customers.

When you create a Look-a-like Audience, you choose a source
audience (a Custom Audience created with information pulled from
your pixel, mobile app, or fans of your Page). Facebook identifies
the common qualities of the people in it (for example, demographic
information or interests). Then, they deliver your ad to an audience
of people who are similar to (or "look like") them.

*https://www.facebook.com/business/help/164749007013531?id=40
1668390442328

Organic Traffic: Content Marketing

According to Moz, on average, *71.33% of searches result in a page
one organic click. Pages two and three get only 5.59% of the clicks.

*https://moz.com/blog/google-organic-click-through-rates-in-2014

This means that only 25-30% of page one clicks come from pay per
click ads. So, if you are not using AdWords, then you are relying
100% on being found organically. With this in mind, what is YOUR
organic marketing strategy?

Content Marketing Defined

According to Wikipedia, content marketing is all about creating and distributing relevant and valuable content to acquire and retain customers. The strategy behind content marketing is to create interest in a product or service through educational, entertaining, or informative material. Successful content marketing relies material. Successful content marketing relies on consistent, high-quality content.

Done well, content marketing not only helps educate and attract customers, but it also helps you show up on page one of Google and other search engines. Plus, it helps you engage readers and drive more traffic to your site.

When it comes to content marketing, I strongly suggest that you don't sell a product, but rather, "sell the click." Basically, you should focus on selling the next step in the buying process. As a successful content marketer, your main objective is to get the Internet searcher off Google and onto your website.

With the main goal of ranking as high as you can on Google SERPS, high-quality content is a must, and the best way to get the click that sends customers and prospects to your website.

Different Types of Content Marketing.

Education Based Marketing: Building Trust
Education Based Marketing is a powerful marketing strategy that helps you establish trust and credibility with messaging that informs or educates. This is in direct contrast to more traditional marketing, which is selling-based.

Education Based Marketing is about helping prospects or customers better understand something, while engaging them just enough to find out where they are in the buying process.

Education Based Marketing reduces fear and distrust, establishing a relationship that encourages a willingness to buy. The more you educate your prospect, the more you build a relationship of trust and respect that dispels their concerns.

Typical Buyer Concerns (We mentioned some of these in the previous section on developing your USP:

- Spas are hard to maintain
- I have to use too many chemicals
- Pools cost a lot to operate
- All dealers say their pools and spas are the best
- What happens if I buy the wrong the spa?
- What happens if I don't like the color?
- What happens if I want to move my spa?
- I'm afraid I'll pay too much

Types of Education Based Marketing Content to Address Buyer Concerns:

- Buyer's Guides
- Stats
- Blogs
- Infographics
- Videos

Education Based Marketing is the perfect way to encourage prospects and customers who are hungry for knowledge about why they need or should want a hot tub or pool. Most of them are looking for reassurance that they're making the right decision. Existing customers want answers to questions like:

"How do I fix "x"?"
"Where can I find "x"?
"What does "x" cost?"

User-Generated Content (UGC)
User Generated Content is one of the more popular types of content marketing strategies. The classic example is customer reviews, which are free! Free in the sense that you do not pay for reviews. But there's a "catch": you must sell something to someone or provide a service that is good enough that they want to take the time to leave you a review.

However, once you do get a review, whether it's on Facebook, Google, or your website, maximize it! Don't make the mistake of getting a great review, only to let it sit there. Put it to work by promoting it on your website, store and on social media.

There are hidden benefits of UGC and customer reviews. Unlike traditional content, UGC is:

- New
- Fresh
- Free
- Great for Social Media
- Great website content
- Helpful with SEO

With content and especially SEO, a variety of strategies used in combination can have a dramatic effect. Reviews are one of those strategies that many SEO experts believe can help your business rank higher in the Google My Business section of the search results.

Other Types of Content Marketing.

Memes
Memes are trendy content strategies that involve finding a meaningful picture and putting useful content on it. There are several meme sites where you can find promotional, funny, cute things with a serious message.

Facebook

On Facebook, it's easy to share traditional information like a photo, or live streaming. You can also create a Facebook 'event', do text messaging, and even receive phone calls. However, if you want to share a video or upload a photo, you must have that content.

Facebook is not just for posting or for advertising. There are a variety of other things you can do that are fun and informative, like creating a 360 video and adding it to both your website and your Facebook page. This type of video allows the user to use the computer mouse to scroll around the area for a virtual tour of whatever your video is showing.

Contest

Some businesses run contests, and many have been very successful. Contests can be another mode to create UGC.

Newsjacking

Newsjacking involves looking at current events and how to tie your products and services to that news event. For example, this past year there was a meteor shower. If you happened to have a photo of your product with stars in the background, and wrote some creative content, that would be the perfect newsjacking opportunity.

Newsjacking doesn't sell your product per se. But it links your business to a popular event, creating a new and different reason to promote your products and services.

Customer Reviews & Testimonial Videos

Many businesses use testimonials and review videos on their websites. And it's free promotion. You can also re-purpose written reviews into video reviews by taking written content and turning it into video content. This gives more weight to the original written review because video is more viral.

It's not enough to simply create great videos, you also need to amplify and promote your content. One place to do that is on social media.

A video review can either be uploaded directly to Facebook and it can reside there, or you can link it to your website, or to YouTube. This is a great way to promote yourself with testimonials and third-party endorsements.

Video Content Marketing
Creating and promoting videos is a smart way to connect better with your visitors. Videos help you stand out from your competitors in a more personal and visual manner. In addition to improved personal connections, when you upload your videos to YouTube and use the embed code to place the video on your website, you get the SEO benefit of a link from YouTube.

Plus, you don't need fancy video equipment to create a great video. Many dealers use a smart phone to create video – many believe this format helps them connect better with their customers with messages that are more believable.

The possibilities with video are endless! Here are a few different types to consider:
- About Us
- Testimonials
- Product Demos
- Website Intros
- Promotional Videos

Blogging
A blog is basically just an article posted to the 'blog' section of your website. The subject matter can be about anything related to your products and services. Be careful not to post promotions and sales through your blog. Blogs should be used only to help establish you and your business as an authority in your market, not for direct selling.

Done right, blogs give your customers and prospects helpful information, while providing the search engines with recent and relevant content. Blogs are interactive too, as you can easily solicit comments and feedback from your readers, which is considered user generated content.

Press Release Marketing
Using a press release is a practical way to broadcast important events or announcements about your business.

There are many things you can write about, including:
- Trends
- Awards
- Contests
- Tips lists
- Milestones
- Holiday Tie-ins
- Human Interest
- Grants and Gifts
- Polls and Surveys
- Health and Medical Issues

After You Create Content, It's Time to *Amplify It!*

Now that you've created an amazing blog post, press release, video, etc., the next step is to make sure as many people see it as possible. You want to amplify your message, extending it beyond just your website.

Social Media Channels.
Social media is a great vehicle to promote your message. Facebook, Instagram, Pinterest and of course YouTube are some of the best and most popular social channels to promote your content. Google My Business now lets you post content and events for a limited time. Even LinkedIn can be a solid place to post information, although I don't suggest you post sales promotions on LinkedIn.

When amplifying content on social media, be sure to have compelling photos and headlines – yes, you need to test different headlines to find the winners.

It's also helpful to post at different times of the day because people tend to check Facebook at different times of the day. Some people check Facebook only in the morning and that's it. Others will check later in the afternoon or multiple times throughout the day.

So, if you post a variety of content at different times of the day, you're likely to capture far more people. It's also a good idea to link your Facebook page to Twitter for automatic reposting. This way, So, every time you post content on Facebook, it will automatically post the same content on Twitter.

E-mail & Newsletters.

Another way to amplify your content is through newsletters. A great newsletter keeps you "top of mind". I subscribe to several newsletters from business owners across the country, but all I seem to see is promotional e-mails – a Father's Day sale, July 4th sale, Mother's Day, Memorial Day etc. Unfortunately, there's nothing educational in the newsletter, just sell, sell, sell.

It's a better strategy to send newsletters even when you're not selling anything. On my newsletter, I show the first paragraph of a new blog post. This way, if my subscribers wish to continue reading the article, they must click, and it sends them directly to the expanded article on my website.

The goal with a newsletter is to get interested visitors to move from an emailed newsletter to your website. Once they arrive at your site, they'll be able to see who you are and what you do.

RSS Feed.
The RSS Feed, which stands for Really Simple Syndication, may not be as relevant as it has been in the past, but it still gives users the ability to subscribe to a blog, and then read it via automated updates. It's similar to a newsletter, except that people don't have to sign up and give you their name and email address.

If you have a blog, especially a WordPress blog, talk to your webmaster to be sure that you have an RSS feed enabled. If you have a WordPress site and want to know if you have a feed, the address is normally something like, www.yourwebsiteaddress.com/feed. If you don't have WordPress site, ask your website developer what the website and the blog feed is, and if they can put that on your website.

You can also post, distribute, or amplify content on Pinterest, YouTube, and many other sites. There are tons of bookmarking sites out there that can also help you.

Push Notifications (for more details, see the expanded section on push notifications).
Push notification marketing is an advertising, communication and re-engagement strategy that lets dealers send messages to customers through clickable browser notifications even when they are not on your website.

Marketers can use these notifications to send out promotional, informational, or educational messages. Push notifications are a great vehicle to inform users about new products, current sales, or even recently published blog posts. In addition, many companies use them as reminders that specific promotions are starting or almost ending, giving readers the motivation to take advantage of the limited savings available to them.

Fine Tuning Your "After the Click" Content Strategy

You've written great content, posted it on social media with wonderful headlines, and you're getting the clicks. You've done everything right up to this point. Don't stop there! Once you get people to engage and click on your link, then what happens? What is your "after-the-click" strategy? What is your follow up system? Is it an automated system like Infusionsoft or Salesforce? Is it semi-automated? Is it phone calls? (see section on)

At this point, you want to establish goals that will help you measure your success. Here are the key questions you must answer about your content marketing.

- What are your goals?
- Why are you even doing it?
- Is to educate, to entertain?
- Who is going to do it?
- How often are you going to do it?
- Do you have the right tools and people to execute it?
- How will you measure your success?
- What is your budget?
- Where will you post it?
- How will you amplify it?

Marketing Tools & Resources.
One easy marketing tool is *Answer the Public,* an online answer generator. You simply type in a keyword, and it returns all the relevant keyword phrases in the form of a question (who, what, when, where, and why) related to your query.

For instance, when I type in the keyword "*hot tubs*", it returned dozens of questions such as:

- How much do hot tubs costs?
- How to clean a hot tub?
- Why hot tubs foam up?
- Why my hot tub water is cloudy?
- Are hot tubs good for diabetes?

This is a great place to start when looking to generate ideas to educate customers. HubSpot is another marketing tool that features a 'Blog Topic Generator'. Type in a few nouns, and it quickly returns suggested blog topics.

Organic Content Marketing Checklist

Step 1 - Create Quality Content to Promote.

- Articles
- Blogs
- Videos
- Infographics
- Images
- Press Releases
- Testimonials
- Podcasts
- Buyer's Guides

Step 2 – Use Off-Site Paid and Organic SEO Strategies to Promote Your Content and Drive Traffic.

- AdWords
- Facebook Advertising
- Retargeting
- Social Media Marketing
- Video Marketing
- Press Release Marketing
- Classified Ads – Craigslist
- Directory Listings – Merchant Circle, Manta
- E-Mail Marketing

Off-Site SEM - Ongoing Strategy Examples

- Video marketing
- Social media
- AdWords (PPC)
- Press release
- Review sites
- Houzz

- Local directories
- Citations
- Google My Business
- Link building
- Newsletters
- E-mail marketing
- Image sites
- Infographics

Google My Business (GMB)

Why Is Google My Business So Important for Your Business?

- GMB search results can appear above organic rankings
- Prospects can see your physical location – inside and out
- All your contact information is prominent and easy to find
- Listing shows your business hours – day by day
- Prospects can see your star rating and read reviews
- Anyone can get directions to your store
- GMB has a direct link to your website
- The GMB listing drives traffic to your business
- Mobile listing has click to call, directions, website link

The 10 Best Ways to Optimize Your GMB Listing

1. Claim and verify your business
2. Select the best categories for your business.
3. Complete the listing100%.
4. The name, address, and phone number (NAP) must match what is on your website.
5. Use a local phone number versus an 800 number
6. Make sure the map location is correct
7. Add photos and videos
8. Update open days and times
9. Get reviews and citations
10. Update regularly, post regularly

How Does Google Decide to Rank Each Listing?
Although no one knows for sure the exact algorithms used, there are several factors that we can infer based on the writing of GMB experts. These include relevance, distance, and prominence.

- *Relevance*: trying to match the listing to the keywords typed in for the search.
- *Distance:* how far each potential search result is from the location term used in the search.
- *Prominence*: how well-known a business is and how much information Google has on the business from citations, posts, and other local directories.

There are many SEO companies that try and figure out GMB ranking factors. One company talked about keywords in the business title, NAP consistency, how many links inbound and outbound, reviews, the quantity of reviews, the review diversity, and social signals.

Enhancing Your Google My Business Listing.
The more things that you can do to enhance your Google My Business listing the better your chances are of ranking higher.

Create Local Citations
    A local citation is the name, address, and phone number for a local business. Citations can occur on local business directories, websites, or apps. The more citations that appear across the Internet that match the NAP of your GMB listing, the better. Examples include Merchant Circle, YP.com, Yellow Pages, etc.

Add an Appointments Tab
    When a user clicks on an appointments tab, it takes them to a *Contact Us* page where they can make an appointment for your business.

Encourage Reviews.
Reviews are great for your business and are said to help your GMB rankings (see reviews section). But regardless of how many five-stars reviews you have, it's not enough! A recent *BrightLocal survey found that for a typical business, 70% of respondents said that the reviews had to be within 30 days (to be meaningful).

*https://www.brightlocal.com/research/local-consumer-review-survey/

Bottom line? You need to continuously get more reviews in both quality and quantity. In the same survey, when asked, "How many online reviews do you read before you can trust a business?", 70% of respondents said four or more.

Responding to Google Reviews.
How do you respond to Google reviews? First, you should ALWAYS respond to reviews – good or bad. When you respond, it signals to Google (or any review site you're on), that there is interaction, and it is not a fake review.

But don't make the mistake of copying and pasting a response to a review. Get personal and mention the reviewer's name in your response. This sends positive signals to Google and Yelp that the review was left by a real person, not an automated bot.

How to Contest a Review*.
Sometimes, it becomes necessary to contest a review. Here's how to do it. Go to Google My Business and click on 'Help'. Then click on 'Flag This Review'. Submit a reason why you think the review is fake or a disgruntled employee.

*https://support.google.com/business/answer/4596773?hl=en&ref_to pic=6109360

How to Get Google My Business Support.
Support is available through Google My Business 'Help'. Once there, you will see a variety of things that you can do to enhance your business.

GMB Help
*https://support.google.com/business/?hl=en#topic=4539639

GMB Insights
*https://support.google.com/business/answer/7069123?hl=en

Flag Inappropriate GMB Reviews
*https://support.google.com/business/answer/4596773?hl=en&ref_to
pic=6109360

Geo-Fencing

Geo-fencing (also referred to as location-based targeting) is a way to target people based on a specific location and then display ads for your product on their smartphones or tablets.

For example, as a hot tub dealer, you might have a new product line you'd like to promote or maybe you're having an anniversary sale. You could spend thousands of dollars on television commercials, online ads, social media, and newspaper ads, blasting your message to everyone in a 20-mile radius.

Or you could focus more of your efforts on people who you know are in the market for your product. Geo-fencing allows you to do this because it draws a virtual fence around a location, and lets you advertise to people who have visited that specific location.
Types of places you can draw a geo-fence around include:

- Competitor locations
- Convention centers
- Tradeshows
- Retail stores
- Malls
- Events

- Your own locations
- High income neighborhoods

The size of your geo-fence can be fairly large, and it can also be as narrow as a 25-foot radius. This precision means you can even target households. If you have a mailing list of new home buyers, residents with high-income levels or event attendees, you could potentially draw a geo-fence around addresses and target the residents of those homes individually.

How Does Geo-Fencing Work?
Geo-fencing works by drawing a virtual line around an area using latitudinal and longitudinal coordinates. The technology is so precise that it can include the contours of a building without wasting ad spend on people directly outside of the building. Also, geo-fencing requires no physical equipment.

When a potential customer with a smartphone or tablet enters a geo-fenced location, GPS technology captures their mobile device ID. While they're at that spot as well as after they leave, your business can show them ads on their mobile devices. There are only two requirements:

1. The user must have location services enabled on their device. Fortunately, about 90% of people leave their location services on because it allows them to use location-based apps like Google maps.

2. They must open a participating app or browse the Internet for your ads to be shown.

Since most people use their smartphones several times a day, the chances are good that your prospect could see your ad while they're at your competitor's store or at an event where they're looking at products just like what you offer. Imagine if you could make them walk out of a competitor's store and drive directly to your place of business!

If they don't use their phones in the geo-fenced area, you'll still be able to remind them about your business for the next 30 days. Since it can take several touch points to make a sale, being able to get repeat exposure can make a world of difference in your sales!

Geo-fencing can also be set up at your store. So, if a potential customer walks in, browses, chats with one of your sale team members, but then leaves, you'll be able to target them with ads. You could show them more of the product line, advertise a discount or offer them a free consultation.

What are the Benefits of Geo-Fencing?
In today's competitive landscape, companies need an edge in order to stand out. It can be a challenge to keep up with the latest and greatest marketing tools, especially in Internet marketing. Geo-fencing is a powerful and cost-effective way to get more customers and grow quickly.

Here are seven of the top benefits:

1. *More precise location targeting.* The area can be as specific as the inside of a building.

2. *Intent-based targeting.* Unlike an ad on television or social media, geo-fencing is showing your product to people who are either already looking for it or are likely to be receptive to the idea of purchasing.

3. *You can market yourself at events even if you're not there.* Tradeshows and events are expensive to attend, and you can't be everywhere all at once. However, with geo-fencing, you can show your products to people at these events. It's like having a virtual booth!

4. *Measure both online and offline conversions.* Other advertising channels are difficult to measure. For example, if someone saw an ad on television and then bought your product, you wouldn't know that the TV advertisement was

responsible for the sale unless they specifically told you. That's because they could have heard an ad on the radio, been referred by a friend or maybe they were just walking by your business. With geo-fencing, you'll know if a specific phone was in your targeted area and then entered your store.

5. *High ROI*. Because the targeting is so specific, many clients find that this marketing channel provides a high return on investment.

6. *Video ads are an option, too*. Therefore, it's just like TV, but more targeted and less costly.

7. *Simple to implement*. There's no equipment needed. Unlike an in-store beacon that requires a piece of hardware that connects to a Bluetooth device, a geo-fence is 100% virtual.

The end result is more efficient marketing spend with ads that are delivered to people who have the intent to buy. And, because the ad window is 30 days, you can provide multiple touchpoints while also reaching out to people who left your store without buying. It's like multiplying the size of your salesforce and allowing them to be everywhere all at once!

So far, we've explained what geo-fencing is and the benefits. It might also be helpful for you to understand what a geo-fencing solution does not do.

Here's what it is not:

- *It's not beacon technology*. A beacon is a physical piece of hardware installed at a location that communicates with devices using Bluetooth. A geo-fence can be installed anywhere because it has no equipment.

- *There are no push notifications or text messaging*. While sending someone an announcement or a coupon for your business as soon as someone visits a competitor might sound good in theory, it's invasive, perceived as spam and can be a customer turn-off. As you might imagine, people could also find it creepy. Geo-fencing, on the other hand, is unobtrusive.

Instead of feeling like they're being stalked or aggressively sold to, your customers are more likely to react with, "Wow, I was just thinking of getting a pool or hot tub. And this company's ad is showing me a new style that I really love. I should get in touch with them. What excellent timing!"

As a result of geo-fencing, the right customers are seeing the right product at the right time.

- ***They are not text ads.*** They are images or video. This is helpful because you can show your product in the best possible light and provide more information than you could in a simple text-based ad.

What Results Can I Expect?
Results will vary, and making promises is impossible. However, there are several case studies of businesses just like yours who have used this marketing tactic with great success. They've seen impressive boosts in foot traffic and sales that are directly attributable to their geo-fencing campaigns.

Is Geo-Fencing Right for Your Business?
Geo-fencing isn't right for all businesses. For example, companies serving a broad, general audience with a low-priced product aren't likely to see success with geo-fencing.

Where we tend to the see the best results is in a market that has a handful of competitors who are selling a high-ticket item that requires research and maybe even in-person selling. Given the price points of hot tubs and in-ground pools, businesses that sell these products can reasonably expect to see positive results with this type of campaign.

Step 4

Convert Traffic into Leads

You Know the Main Purpose of Your Website, Right?

- A place for online consumers can find you.
- Positioning your business as the expert in the area.
- Establish credibility.
- An online brochure.
- To educate prospects about why they should buy from you.
- To support company image and provide customer service.

While all the above is true, it is just a means to an end. **There is only one main purpose for your website and that is to convert website visitors into leads.** Everything else that you do is to support generating leads and ultimately converting leads into sales. Think in these terms when you're building your website or talking to a web designer.

Calls to Action are an Absolute Necessity

Promotions and sales attract today's buyers, that's the low-hanging fruit. The question is, what are you doing to convert <u>future</u> buyers? What are you doing to fill the top of your sales funnel? Remember, you must fill your sales funnel constantly. After all, if you never do anything to convert website visitors into leads, you're not filling your sales funnel.

Attract buyers at the top of the sales funnel with "calls to action" for every type of prospect. Common requests from prospects are:

- Pricing
- Buyer's guide
- Brochures
- Service
- Finding the Perfect Hot Tub

What is a Website "Call to Action"?
While there are varied opinions on what makes effective digital marketing strategy and technique, when it comes to the "call to action", or CTA, the definition is clear. A CTA is simply a button or link on a webpage that drives prospective leads to take some further action.

In many ways, a CTA is a "next step" in the buying cycle that creates a link between content being consumed and additional content where users are prompted to fill out a form, provide an email address or take some further action. A typical website CTA may include descriptive phrases like "Click here" or "Download now" for example.

What are the Characteristics of a Winning Call to Action?
A great CTA isn't necessarily difficult to create, but there are common traits that the very best share. Best practices have identified several features of CTAs that work. Here are a few characteristics of winning CTAs that get the click.

CTA's need to contain an action verb such as: Get, Request, Click, Download, Call (Get Price, Request Quote, Download Guide, Call Now). In addition, CTAs should be:

- Visually appealing
- Short and concise
- Active voice, not passive
- Communicate a sense of urgency

- Reside at the top of every page, or logical end point
- Easy to find and read

Typical Calls to Action that You Should Consider Adding to Your Website.

Hot Tubs
- Get Pricing
- Find Your Perfect Hot Tub
- Download Hot Tub Buyer's Guide
- Get Service
- Take a Test Soak
- Request In-Home Consultation
- Get Hot Tub Brochure

Swim Spas
- Get Pricing
- Find Your Perfect Swim Spa
- Download Swim Spa Buyer's Guide
- Get Service
- Take a Test Soak
- Request Backyard Consultation
- Get Swim Spa Brochure

Saunas
- Get Pricing
- Find Your Perfect Sauna
- Download Sauna Buyer's Guide
- Get Service
- Take a Test Soak
- Request In-Home Consultation
- Get Sauna Brochure

Pools
- Get Pricing
- Find Your Perfect Above Ground Pool
- Download Pool Buyer's Guide
- Get Service
- Request Backyard Consultation
- Open My Pool
- Close My Pool

Live Chat & Messenger Marketing

When you look at your current inbound and outbound Internet marketing strategies it probably includes a mix of pay-per-click (PPC) like Google AdWords and Facebook ads. If you're more aggressive, you might also be using video marketing, blogging, e-mail newsletters, Instagram, and on-site search engine optimization (SEO). But the reality is that most of your competitors are using these strategies too.

Everyone uses these marketing strategies because there hasn't been anything really new since social media became a "thing" in 2008! Until now. Introducing Messenger Marketing.

What is Messenger Marketing for Hot Tub Dealers and Pool Builders?
Messenger marketing (sometimes referred to as conversation marketing) is an effective way to communicate with prospects and customers either in real time (via live chat) or through an automated chat system 24 hours a day, 7 days a week.

Messenger marketing is conversational, interactive and offers your website visitors a method of instant communication in which they are in control of the over interaction. These conversations can take place via mobile apps like WhatsApp or WeChat or through Facebook Messenger. And according to Social Media Today, 1.3 billion people use Facebook Messenger on a monthly basis

Is "Live Chat" Considered Messenger Marketing?
In some ways, yes and in a "perfect world" you would offer live chat 24/7 with customer service agents always available to answer customer and prospect questions.

Unfortunately, that's not a real option for most dealers. There are many free live chat options to use on your website, so price isn't the problem in deciding to use live chat.

The problem most dealers have with offering live chat is they need a person(s) dedicated to managing these live interactions in real time. That means your employees need to stop whatever they're doing regardless of how important it is to chat with someone asking a question that may not be time sensitive like "how late are you open today?"

Common Reasons Why Consumers Get Frustrated with Live Chat:

- No one is online and available even though the live chat is on
- No one is available when consumers typically shop – before and after normal business hours
- Many websites require consumers to fill out a form to even start a live chat
- Companies that take too long to respond

When Offering Live Chat, Dealers Have Several Options:

- Don't offer it and miss out on a great way to interact with customers and prospects – not a good option
- Turn on live chat and sporadically interact whenever you can – again, not a good option
- Offer live chat, but only turn it on when you can have a person available – better than option 2, but confusing for scheduling your employees and website visitors
- Use a combination live chat/automated chat system that answers question 24/7 using live chat when you are available and automation when you're not

What Are the Benefits of Using Live Chat, Chatbots & Messenger Marketing?

Close Sales Faster
Unlike email marketing, customers see Messenger marketing more as a conversation, versus a marketing campaign. And, unlike email marketing, customers want and expect you to interact with them at conversation speed. Therefore, they don't think twice if you send messages every 10-15 seconds instead of every few days.

Doing this via a chatbot or in real time allows you to show the prospect the benefits of your products, give them a discount to prompt them to buy, and help generate a highly qualified lead within minutes instead of days.

Generate Higher Quality Leads More Easily
By using the Facebook Messenger platform in conjunction with an automated chat, the moment a prospect clicks on either your website or Facebook "Get Started" chat button, they have just "opted-in." This means you now have instant access to the information they've shared about themselves on Facebook, i.e.: name, email, phone number, etc. with no forms to fill out or other info to capture.

Boost Customer Satisfaction 24/7
As a hot tub and pool dealer, you likely struggle to always meet customer demand for support. While large brands offer 24/7 support, this might put a strain on your business. Messenger marketing provides help without the added staff and costs.

Use Chatbots as an Interactive Call to Action

Chatbots are interactive software programs that can be used to automatically engage with messages they receive. Depending on how you set them up, Chatbots can be programmed to respond the exact same way each time they are engaged or to respond differently to messages they get that contain specific targeted keywords.

Chatbots can be deployed in several different ways, but most frequently are found using mobile phone SMS text, website chat and on social media sites like Facebook and Twitter.

Chatbots are becoming more accepted by people of all ages therefore more companies are using them in a variety of different ways. The most frequent things that shoppers like about using chatbots are:

- Getting quick answers to questions at any time of day
- Inquiring about the different types of products and services you offer
- Getting more specs and details about a specific product model
- Getting in touch with a live sales, service, or customer service representative

What Can Chatbots Actually Do?

Interact with Prospects and Customers
Because current customers and prospective clients initially interact with a chatbot, by the time the sales or service teams get involved, the chatbots have already initiated a conversation, answered some frequently asked questions and are now ready to engage with a live person.

Pre-Qualify Buyers
By providing answers to prospective buyer's frequently asked questions, leads can be segmented into specific product or service categories thus providing your sales or service team useful information to expedite the sales process.

Automate Frequently Asked Questions
Most customers that find your business on Facebook or land on your website are looking for specific answers. Most often they are quick questions like: What are your hours? Where are you located? Do you offer service? Can you fix my Widget?

These are the types of questions where chatbots can get your customers the information they need instantly 24 hours a day, 7 days a week. Using chatbots in this way can free up a significant amount of time for your employees.

Enhance Your other Marketing and Promotion Strategies
Whether you are using Facebook or Google Ads, direct mail, e-mail marketing or just website promotions, Chatbots can eventually turn all your outbound marketing efforts into lead generating interactive conversations

More Benefits of Using Chatbots.

Website Lead Generation
Having a "live chat" pop-up on your website is great **IF** you have a live person dedicated to being on call during normal working hours, but how many business owners have the personnel to do this? Not many! And nothing is more frustrating to a customer or prospect than using a live chat only to find out that no one is live and ready to answer their questions.

Chatbots to the rescue! Having a chatbot pop-up is a great way start a conversation with website visitors and answer frequently asked questions all without having a live person initially involved. If the website visitor engages with your chatbot and needs more information that is not provided, they always have the option to request a live person. In this way you have an employee who is "on-call" and can interact with a customer as needed versus a full-time live chat person.

Facebook Lead Generation
If you are not using Facebook Messenger Chatbots yet on your business page, you may want start. It is growing in popularity and can quickly and easily answer questions and engage customers and prospects.

You can use a Facebook chatbot to:

- Have a welcome message on your business page and provide frequently asked questions (FAQs) to engage users to "Get Started."
- Send and receive texts and photos and include specific calls to action sending users to a specific landing page on your website
- Offer a variety of detailed options about your products and services and let users select what's important to them.
- Provide users with the opportunity to contact a live person at your company

Facebook also offers a few different types of Messenger ads. When they tap on an ad, they'll be sent to the destination you chose during ads creation - whether that's a specific page on your website site or a conversation with your business right on Messenger. Visitors can also start a text conversation with your business using the "Send Message" button option.

24/7 Customer Support
Installing a chatbot on your Facebook page or on your website allows you to offer at least some level of customer service even when your business is closed.

Start Conversations with Customers/Prospects in a Fun/Unique Way
Phone calls and emails are still effective but offering chat as an option to your customers and prospects is fast, easy, unique, and even fun for many. Plus, it also offers yet another way for people to communicate with you on their terms. It may also set you apart from your competition who do not offer his option yet.

Help Customers and Prospects "Find Their Way"
Many first-time buyers may know they want to buy your product, but which one? Will it meet their specific needs and budget? Size, colors, options, add-ons, accessories, financing can all be very confusing

A great way to use chatbots is to ask a series of qualifying questions that will eventually send your prospect to the page on your website where they can find the information they need to make an informed buying decision.

Are Chatbots Right for Your Business?
Seriously, I can't think of a reason not to use chatbots. Will every customer or prospect use them? Of course not. But for those that do, it can lead to more/better more engagement, answer questions quickly and easily, qualify prospects and of course generate more leads for your business.

The most important part of using chatbots is to make sure it is set up correctly right from the start. Here are just a few things you need to think about:

Strategy
- What should I use the chatbot for?
- What do I want to accomplish?
- Who am I trying to reach?

Set Up
- How should I set up the chatbot flow?
- What will the automated conversation Q&A look like?
- When should I offer the "live" option?
- Who is going to write all the content?
- Can I use photos, videos, and links or just text?
- Should I use it just on Facebook or just my website or both?

Customers and Prospects
- What information do my customers and prospects want?
- How will I deliver this information?

Other
- How will I measure the effectiveness of the chatbot?
- How soon can I get started?
- How soon before I see results?
- Can the chatbot flows be changed once implemented?

Web Push Notification Marketing

Push notification marketing is an advertising, communication and re-engagement strategy that will let dealers send messages to customers and through clickable browser notifications even when they are not on your website anymore.

Marketers can use these notifications to send promotional, informational, or educational messages. Push notifications are a great vehicle to inform users about new products, current sales, or even recently published blog posts. In addition, many companies use them as reminders that specific promotions are starting or almost ending giving the readers the motivation to take advantage of the limited savings available to them.

This relatively new marketing strategy allows you to reach out to your previous website visitors even when you don't have traditional contact information like name, email, and phone number. Please note however that these notifications can be sent only to people who have specifically subscribed to get these web push notifications directly from your website.

Why Use Push Notifications?
For one, they offer you another way for to connect with your customers and prospects. In addition, browser push notifications are delivered even when subscribers are not on your website, checking email or texting. Generally, this leads to much higher open rates and user engagement and can drive more traffic back to your website.

If done right, this type of communication can also increase customer retention because you're frequently reaching out to customers and prospects reminding about your products and services before they lose interest and maybe buy somewhere else.

Currently push notifications work on multiple browsers including Google Chrome, Firefox, Edge, and Opera.

How Do Push Notifications Work?

After you install and turn on the necessary software, visitors to your website will then see an opt-in message box asking the user's consent or permission to send him/her future notifications.

Subscribing is super easy...it only takes one click! Subscribers don't need to provide name, email, phone number or any other personal information. After clicking on "allow," the push subscription is saved in the browser to be used later to send web push notifications. Notifications work on both desktop and mobile devices.

Messages are not blocked by ad blockers because subscribers agree to receive notifications through their browser. Therefore, push notifications are not spam and ad blockers won't affect the delivery of your messages.

Push notifications do not rely on cookies. Instead, your browser assigns each user a unique registration key. Users can opt-out by changing their settings

Message Types:

Welcome Message
Just like the best practices when someone opts-in for a call to action or newsletter, you'll want to create a nice welcome message. Then you'll need to thank them for opting in and let them know that you'll be sending them notifications from time to time. You might also want to provide some valuable free information like a buyer's guide or even a discount coupon towards the purchase on their next accessory purchase.

Updates
Recently published blogs, educational videos or even new products and services you offer.

Reminders
Upcoming sales or promotions, time remaining before the current sale ends or even store hours for specific holidays.

Are Push Notifications Right for Your Dealership?
As you already know, only a small percentage of people visiting your website ever end up opting in for any of the information you offer like buyer's guides or price requests. So, the more ways you can engage with your website visitors, the better.

Remember, we should be offering multiple ways to communicate with prospects that are convenient for them, not necessarily us. In addition to e-mail, phone and text, push notifications are just one more option that you should be offering.

Step 5

Convert Leads into Sales

Now that you have a lead and have delivered the information that was requested, how do you follow up and close the sale?

Many/most times it is the job of your sales team to follow up with prospects. Typical follow up methods include e-mail, phone call, newsletters, text/message/chat, direct mail, or some combination of a few of these. In subsequent chapters, you are going to read about a variety of follow up marketing strategies.

Step 5 of the 9 steps to Internet marketing success is obviously critical to increasing sales and growing your business, but since this book is strictly about Internet marketing, we do not go into sales techniques or closing strategies. We feel that is best handled by attending professional sales training provided by your manufacturers.

Step 6

Track Your Website Analytics

How Would You Like to Know...?

- How many people visit your website each month?
- What pages they look at?
- What city they are from, and
- Where they were just before they came to your site?

With Google Analytics You Can!

Google Analytics is a free service provided by Google that provides detailed statistics about your website traffic.

Reviewing specific sections once a month will give you a good overview of how your website is performing in terms of traffic and user experience.

When you sign into Google Analytics, you'll see an overview page that tells you about sessions, users and page views that happened during a specific timeframe.

Key GA Terminology:

- Users = unique visitors.
- Page views = how many pages people viewed on the site.
- Pages per Session = how many pages the average user visited while they were on the site.

- Average Session Duration = how much time the average user spent on the site.
- Bounce Rate = the percentage of single-page sessions. In other words, somebody came to the site, and whatever page they landed on, they did not go deeper than that one page.

Google Analytics provides information on traffic channels, breaking stats down between organic, direct, paid, referral, social, and display and tells you the most visited pages.

What are Your Best Lead Sources?
A lead which in this instance is considered a conversion or goal completion is defined as somebody who has provided you with contact information. Do you know where your best sources of leads come from? You can use Google Analytics to learn the following:

1. Which channels are your best leads coming from? Is it organic or is it paid?

2. Which search engines give you the best leads? Is it organic, AdWords, Google, Bing, or Yahoo?

While Google is the "800-pound gorilla" of search engine leads, Bing still provides high-quality leads. Bing may not deliver a high *quantity* of leads, but the quality is there.

Look to see where your best search engine leads come from, and typically you'll see Google first, followed by Bing (organic), then Yahoo (organic), and finally Bing (PPC).

Desktop vs. Mobile Leads
Are your best leads coming from desktop, mobile, or tablet?

Even though the number of leads captured from tablet and mobile are increasing, the numbers overall are still higher on a desktop (at least at the time of this writing). And remember, it's easier to opt in (fill out a form) for something on a desktop than it is on mobile.

Bottom line, you need to make it easy for someone to opt-in and provide their name and email address on mobile as well as tablet.

What to Do with All This Information?
- Create measurable calls to action on your website
- Review where your best traffic is coming from and adjust your budget accordingly
- Review which traffic sources generate more leads and adjust spending towards your best traffic and lead source
- Reallocate organic versus paid to support traffic sources
- Make sure you have a mobile-friendly site

Get Information on Demographics & Psychographics

Demographics is information about who your visitors are; psychographics is what they do in their spare time, when they're not working. In addition to Google Analytics, on AdWords, you can find your best zip codes and Google will also tell you the top 10 cities. This information can help you target specific geographic areas for both online and offline marketing.

What Can You do with This Information?
- Target top cities on AdWords
- Target top cities and zip codes for organic marketing
- Use laser target remarketing.

Increasing Ad Budget May Not Result in More Leads

Increasing your ad budget isn't a guaranteed way to increase leads and generate sales. If you increase your ad budget, over time, organic traffic tends to go down. That's because many searchers see an ad at the top of the page and just click versus taking the time to scroll down?

It Pays to be Careful.
Can you spend too much on AdWords? I think so, and it can negatively affect organic traffic. This matters since organic is a higher quality of traffic.

Plus, relying on AdWords entirely makes it challenging to develop a strong organic presence for non-PPC prospects.

In fact, only about 25 to 30% of people on Google actually click on ads. Conventional wisdom says that in general, most people want to click on the organic section more than they want to click on ads because they realize what they are – they know the difference between earned versus paid listings. Therefore, it's best to maintain a steady organic marketing strategy throughout the entire year.

Is Facebook Marketing Worth it?

Is all the time and money you spend on Facebook (and other social media) actually paying off? That depends on your objectives. Are you looking to:

- Increase exposure
- Increase engagement
- Drive website traffic
- Lead generation
- Link building
- Other

Check your Google Analytics stats – how much traffic did you get last month from Facebook? How long was the average visit and did any of that traffic actually generate a lead or conversion?

What Can You do with this Information?
- Review social media goals vs. the amount of money spent vs. the ROI.
- Are you doing the right kind of Facebook marketing?
- Allocate marketing budget based on stats.

How to Set Up & Measure Goals, Leads & Conversions

Google AdWords.
Be sure to set up 'goals' in Google Analytics so you can track progress over time. Create multiple goals - one for call to action like product price, buyer's guide etc. Each goal will be measured individually.

It's easy to measure goals and conversions on AdWords. This is an important step, since just measuring clicks and click through rates isn't enough. In other words, you could be generating clicks and traffic but not know if the traffic is generating leads. Being able to track conversions will help you accurately measure the effectiveness of your Google AdWords.

What Should You Do with The Information You Collect?
- Add calls to action to your website
- Set up goals on Google Analytics
- Add conversion tracking to Google AdWords
- Monitor all the above monthly

Google Search Console.
Google Search Console provides even more insight in terms of what Google can measure about your website performance including search queries, technical issues and the number of pages indexed.

What Should You so with the Information You Collect?
- Review your search console stats
- Review any error messages
- Submit a sitemap
- Check your mobile site

Google My Business.
Your Google My Business insights and stats are where you can see customers that viewed your business either by searching on Google or on maps. These are free insights and statistics!

The most common action that prospects take when visiting your Google My Business page is to request directions. You can also see how many people called.

Important! When looking at your Google stats, be sure your name, address, and phone number matches. It's critical that all your directory listings with Google match and that what Google says about your business is what appears on your website.

Citations are listings that appear throughout the internet. Once you are sure that your Google My Business information is correct, you can start posting and update your citations.

Check the stats on your Google My Business page regularly to see what's happening on your page, and to ensure your information is correct or your business will not be found. If your phone number isn't right, potential customers will call the wrong number. And if your address doesn't match, then you're sending people to the wrong spot on the map.

Step 7

The Customer/Prospect Journey

A customer journey is the complete summary of all the experiences that customers or prospects go through when interacting with your company.

It's not just an email, phone call, or a website visit. It's a combination of everything. The customer journey with a company is not linear. Customers and prospects interact with your brand in a variety of different ways, including but not limited to:

- An e-mail message
- Website content
- A phone conversation
- A face-to-face conversation

Therefore, whenever you have a touch point with customers or prospects, it needs to be as good as it can possibly be.

How & When You Should Follow Up with a Customer

The "how" of following up with a customer can only be determined by how much contact information you actually have. If someone has given you a phone number, chances are, they want you to call them. If they've only provided an email, then they are likely only expecting an e-mail.

The "when" of customer engagement is a bit trickier. When a lead conversion comes in from your website, you should have an automated email acknowledging the visitor's request. This email doesn't need to be complicated and can be as simple as "Thank you very much. We've received your request and we'll respond to your needs shortly".

The forms on your website should be set up to not only send automated emails to those who request information, but also to go to the person or team in your company tasked with following up on leads. All leads should be addressed within 24 hours.

3 Rules for a Great Follow Up Conversation.
That first contact with a prospect can feel daunting. But knowing what kind of information to provide is essential.

Rule Number One:
> Always answer questions as directly as possible. For example, when someone asks, "What's the price of your widget?" If you're selling a low-ticket item, respond with, "the price is X dollars".
>
> However, if you're selling a high-ticket item or a service, it's tough to answer because pricing can depend on a variety of factors like size, colors, accessories, delivery, etc. Your best bet is to answer as directly as you can, giving the prospect a price range when possible. This response is always better than not answering a customer question because you're afraid you might scare them away.

Rule Number Two:
> Always provide a next step or identify an action to be taken.

Rule Number Three:
> Always ask how they would like to hear from you. For example, you could ask them, "What's the best way to communicate with you?" or "how do you like to shop?" Asking questions is always good practice and is a smart way to bring the customer closer to you.

What Makes a Good Response *Good*?

- Speed of response
- Answering the question honestly
- Providing helpful information

I can't stress enough the importance of speed when responding to customers. But speed and accuracy of information must go together. It's not enough to send out a bland "non-answer".

When following up on leads, I like to ask clients, "What is your responsibility?" Even better, "What is your "*Response*-ability"? Your ability to respond quickly and effectively to customers will depend entirely on the follow up process that you put in place.

The question now is, what kind of system or process do you currently have in place to respond to all the leads you receive or generate yourself?

Response Processes & The Role of Automation
Why is having effective processes and automation important for your business? Systems and processes are consistent, repeatable, and predictable.

There are many ways to follow up with people:

- E-mail
- Snail mail
- Phone
- Chat
- Messenger
- Text

It's smart to create a process that addresses all of these.

Who Does What, When?
When designing your customer response process, keep the following three questions in mind:

- Who is in charge of following up on the leads in your company?
- What are they supposed to do with the lead?
- How do you measure and monitor their progress and success?

Grow Your Email List & Generate More Leads

Increase Email Open Rates.
It's great that you're sending out email to potential leads. But nothing can happen until your email is opened. So, if you put a lot of time into creating a terrific email, and nobody opens it, it's a waste of time. Luckily, there are a variety of ways that you can increase and improve your chances of having your emails *opened.*

Here are 5 strategies to increase email open rates.

1. Personalize It
Personalized emails improve click-through rates by 14%, and conversion rates by 10%. (Aberdeen Group) After all, you're asking people to give you their name, so why not address them personally in the email? Most email autoresponders have a code where you can insert a first or last name, etc.

2. Create a Captivating Subject Line
Nearly 33% of email recipients open email based on subject line alone. (Convince & Convert via Salesforce.com) I can't tell you how important a great subject line is, to creating an email that gets opened. If a subject line isn't enticing enough, or engaging enough, the recipient is simply not going to open it.

There are several places online to help you craft winning copy, from subject lines to headlines. Popurls.com can help you create interesting subject lines based on what's trending and what people are looking at now. Reddit.com is a similar site, where you might be able to pick up a few more ideas. And there are several tools available to help you analyze headlines for emotional marketing value.

3. Know the Importance of the First Sentence

It's critical that the subject line and first sentence of your email go together. Why? G-mail pulls a portion of the first sentence of your email with the subject line when it appears in your inbox. So, the subject line and first sentence are a great one-two punch.

4. Optimize Performance with Split Testing

Before sending out a newsletter, consider split-testing different subject lines to different portions of your list. This is a quick way to determine which one performs best.

Here's how to do it: Develop two subject lines, subject line A and subject line B. If you have 5000 email recipients, send subject line A to 500 people and subject line B to the remaining 500 people. Apart from the subject lines, the rest of the newsletter is exactly the same. After it has been delivered, look at the stats for each and review the open rates. Take the subject line that works the best and use it to send your newsletter to the remaining contacts on your list.

5. Ensure Email Compatibility

If your email doesn't render well in your recipient's email system, they will have a difficult time understanding it. Luckily, there's a handy alternative that allows subscribers to see your email as it was intended to be viewed. You have the option of adding a message at the top of your email that says something similar to, "having trouble reading this? Click here to open in your browser".

If you're using Emma, Salesforce, or another autoresponder system, this message is essentially boilerplate - another advantage of using an autoresponder versus sending emails out from a service like Outlook.

Of course, you don't want to send individual emails from Outlook when you can send thousands with a professional email sending system!

Monitor Stats to Measure Effectiveness.
Most autoresponders will provide stats once a newsletter or email blast has been sent out. This can include such things as open and click-through rates, and bounce rates. You can also learn whether readers open your email on a mobile device or a desktop.

Apply Segmentation & Lead Nurturing.
Prospects and customers are different and shouldn't receive the same email. For example, you probably don't want to send an email with the subject line "36 months no-interest financing," to someone that just bought last week.

Be sure to segment your list, whether it's between product A and product B or prospects and customers. And remember, there is a difference between newsletters and sales broadcasts. Sending out only promo emails is not lead nurturing. If all people get from you is, "buy, buy, buy," then you are not developing a relationship.

Email Marketing Hacks, Tricks & Tips

Don't Burn Out Your List During Promotions.
A promotional email campaign that drops emails on the 18th, 19th, 21st, 24th, 27th, 29th and the 30th of each month is burning out your list even if you use different subject lines. If the only time people hear from you is when you have a sale, your list is going to tire of you "beating them over the head" with "sale, sale, sale" messages.

Use Symbols/Emojis in Your Description.
Symbols placed strategically in email can be a great way to add visual interest to text. Orbitz does it by using vacation symbols like planes and beach umbrellas. The more attention you can bring to your subject line, the more likely your email will get noticed, opened, and read. Where do you find them? Go to Wikipedia, and you'll find many symbols you can grab and use for free.

Use Animated GIFs.
You can't embed a video into an email, but you can embed an animated GIF (graphic interchange format) or moving image.

When someone opens an email and it blinks, "Click here to claim your rebate" with a moving image, they think, "Oh, gosh, they're saying something and I'm not hearing it." This is a subtle way of compelling people to click. And when they do, they are redirected to a specific landing page with a real video.

Make Your Messages Responsive for Any Screen.
Between 40% to 60% of consumers read emails on smartphones. Therefore, the majority of autoresponders powered by Salesforce, Infusionsoft, etc. make the email message responsive. If you're not sure if your messages are responsive, send an email to yourself ahead of time to check.

Use Multiple Links, Different Texts, Photos & a PS to See Which Converts Most.
Most email services make it easy to identify which of your links get clicked the most. For instance, you might see that 100 people clicked on a specific link, with 93 clicking on the PS, 3 on the GIF and none on the link in the first line.

Create an Effective Landing Page. (see previous section on landing pages)
To create a landing page that works, you need a compelling headline, a sub-headline, a call-to-action, and social proof testimonials. Equally important, your landing page content must match your link and the promise that was made in your email.

Email at the Right Time.
Research by GetResponse.com has identified the specific time of day when people are more likely to click and open emails. The top click and open hours are in the morning, between 8:00 and 9:00, and again between 3:00 and 4:00 in the afternoon.

Step 8

Test, Track Refine and Repeat

One of the least utilized ways to improve your online business is by testing new ideas related to your website and/or Internet marketing strategies. Most dealers make the mistake of thinking that once they build a new website, deploy a new AdWords campaign, start sending out a newsletter or start posting to Facebook, etc. that they're done with that part of their business. Nothing could be further from the truth!

While implementing all these strategies are important, their creation and continued use is only the beginning. Even though you may be getting good results from all of these, you can't assume that the results you are getting today will continue. Consumer preferences change, competitors get smarter and search engines like Google get "smarter" in terms of the results they provide their users.

In addition, just because you saw improvements after creating a new website or starting a new AdWords campaign, doesn't mean that you can't improve upon what you've already done to generate even more traffic, clicks, engagement and leads. The only way to know if you are getting the most out of your marketing efforts is to test everything and then compare it to your previous results. Even small changes can generate big results.

Listed below are many different things you can change, update, or modify to generate more traffic, clicks, and leads. Some are related and cross over into other areas like website copy, headlines, and keyword placement. Others like Facebook ads and AdWords are similar but require different strategies.

Regardless of what you decide to test, be sure to establish a starting benchmark so that you see if your changes made a difference. Stats from Google Analytics and Search Console, advertising stats from AdWords and Facebook as well as open rates and click rates from your autoresponder should be able to give you the starting benchmarks you need. Listed below each section, I included some metrics that can be used to measure the success of any changes you make.

Step-by-Step Testing Procedure

- Decide on your objective (what you want to improve - i.e.: conversions, clicks, etc.)
- Establish your goals - i.e.: 10% increase in traffic
- Select what parts of your website or Internet marketing you are going to test- i.e. – website, newsletters
- Establish your benchmarks- i.e.: – 62% bounce rate
- Decide how long to run each test - i.e. – 3 months
- Make your changes - i.e.: website copy, AdWords headlines
- Accumulate data- i.e.: Google Analytics
- Analyze data- i.e.: Google Analytics – compare previous 3 months or same time from previous year
- Decide if the changes accomplished the goals you set
- Keep, discard, or modify previous changes – i.e.: if it worked, keep it, if not try something else
- Move on to the next set of testing

Website Testing Options

- Colors – headers, background, buttons
- CTAs – page placement, button colors, CTA types, amount of info to request, closing rate
- Design – boxed vs. full screen
- Long scrolling vs. shorter "above the fold" pages
- Pop ups – page placement
- Font types and sizes

- Chat – Live vs. chatbot
- AdWords landing pages
- Facebook landing pages
- Navigation tabs – how many, text, sub menus
- Split Test – A/B home page

Website Stats to Review & Compare.
Number of users, pages per session, bounce rate, time on site, conversions, paid versus organic conversions, site speed, desktop versus mobile traffic, top pages, organic versus paid traffic,

On-Site SEO & Content Testing Options

- Meta titles
- Meta descriptions
- On-page text
- Text length
- Number of pages
- Links – internal and external
- Keywords – for search engines, voice, YouTube
- Keyword placement
- Headlines & copy
- Images
- Videos
- Product descriptions

SEO & Content Stats to Review & Compare.
Number of users, pages per session, bounce rate, time on site, conversions, paid versus organic conversions, site speed, desktop versus mobile traffic, top pages, organic versus paid traffic,

Blogging Testing Options

- How often
- Subjects
- Headlines

- Article length
- Blog types – text, video, combination of text and video, infographics, etc.
- Engagement

Blogging Stats to Review & Compare.
Page views, time on site, scrolling, link clicks, conversions, social media shares, user flow, exit pages

Email Marketing Testing Options

- Personalization – name in subject line and email
- Headlines – short, long
- Message – informative, promotional, aggressive versus passive, CTAs
- Offer types - % discount, $ discount, financing, warehouse, tent, parking lot sale type words
- Opening sentence – aggressive, less aggressive, long versus short
- Photos – product, people, moving gifs, none at all
- Memes – do they improve open rates, clicks, conversion – meme types
- Emoji's – do they improve open rates, clicks, conversion – emoji types
- Email types – html vs text
- Format – email layout templates

Email Marketing Stats to Review & Compare.
Open rates, clicks, devices used, link clicks, conversions, time on site

AdWords Testing Options

- Ads
- Ad types – text versus graphic, dynamic, video, Gmail
- Headlines
- Display URL
- CTRs
- Conversions
- Keywords
- Keywords vs. search terms
- Negative keywords
- Landing pages - CTAs, colors, actual offer
- On page text – headlines, formatting – bullet points, white space
- Keyword match types – broad vs. exact
- Geo targeting types – radius, zip code, county, city

AdWords Stats to Review & Compare.
Click through rate (CTR), cost per click, conversions, conversion rate, quality score, desktop vs. mobile traffic, top pages

Social Media Testing Options

- Facebook ad types, objectives
- Geo-targeting
- Budget, audience, placement
- Optimization and delivery
- Post types - video, photos, carousel
- Time of day
- Frequency
- Amount of text

Social Media Stats to Review & Compare.
Website traffic, Facebook insights using pixel, likes, link clicks, engagement, and conversions.

Step 9

The Value of a Great Referral

Every small business owner knows that referrals are the best way to get customers. Referrals from current customers come predisposed to do business with you because a friend or someone they trust referred them.

In fact, many small business owners say that referrals bring them the highest returns when compared to other traditional marketing methods, such as advertising, direct mail, and networking.

When 30% to 50% of your business comes through referrals, your business becomes self-sustaining, allowing you to focus more on value added efforts, like expanding your product and service offerings.

Referrals are powerful because they come from a credible third-party that has experienced first-hand the benefits of doing business with you.

They're even more powerful when they come from a friend, because friends typically don't have ulterior motivations, but wish to do what's in your best interest. It's often easier to believe what a friend says versus hearing a commercial or listening to a salesperson whose sole purpose is to make money.

Referrals are also valuable because most of the time they are completely free. How would you like to receive the benefits of the most compelling sales advertisement on earth for absolutely nothing? You can through referrals.

Finally – and I think this is the most powerful reason of all - customers that give referrals become more loyal to you and your business. Why? Once someone stands up and makes a public statement about something – whether it's positive or negative – they tend to become twice as committed. If you can get your customers to go on record endorsing your products, store, or services, they're likely to become more loyal to you and your business.

Before You Set Up Your Referral Marketing System, You Need to be Sure Your Business Worthy of Being Referred!

- Are you delivering on your promises?
- Are you exceeding expectations?
- Are you thanking your customers for their business?
- Are your products and services better than the competition?
- Do you have the WOW factor?

Without going into too much detail on the 5 areas listed above, I will say this: to thrive in any business, you MUST deliver great products and services and do it in a way that "wows" you customers.

Word-of-Mouth vs. Referral Systems

I often get calls from business owners looking for marketing advice. The very first question I ask them is, "How do you get clients right now?" Almost always, the answer is, "mostly from referrals". My next question is, "How do you go about getting referrals?"

After a long pause, the usual response is, "Well, nothing really. People usually know what I do, and they refer their friends to me." That sounds great, but let's be honest – this is the WORST way to get referrals.

Let me explain what I mean. When people refer others to you, it is commonly called, "Word-of-Mouth" marketing. While word-of-mouth marketing is good, referrals normally come to you in a very haphazard way.

Two people start talking about a problem and one person happens to know you and the problem just happens to be something that this person knows you're good at solving so they mention the name of your company.

The Importance of Creating a Word-of-Mouth System.
As just mentioned, most word-of-mouth referrals happen by chance – there's nothing methodical or systematic about it. And, even worse, the chances of it happening consistently are slim. In fact, if you're currently getting all your referrals through word-of-mouth marketing, you're probably only getting a small percentage of the referrals that you could and should be receiving.

If you want to survive in any type of economy, you can't rely on word-of-mouth marketing as the sole way of getting referrals. It's simply not enough. To be clear, your business *needs* word-of-mouth referrals, but it also needs a referral marketing <u>system</u>. As you know, systems are what make so many franchises successful.

Think about this: why are everyday franchises like McDonalds® so successful? Because they have developed systems that work. Make no mistake, people who buy a McDonalds franchise are not buying hamburgers, they're buying a program that has proven the test of time. They are buying a successful system!

That's why the most successful franchises cost so much. They've laid out your success plan in detail. Do what they tell you to do – "connect the dots", "paint by their numbers," etc., and odds of success increase dramatically. It just makes sense to follow their success formula.

You need to do the same for your referrals in your company – create a system! By creating a referral marketing system, valuable, money-making referrals will happen in a more systematic, reliable, and predictable way.

This sounds easy, so why don't more business owners have a referral marketing system in place? The answer is that most of us get caught up in the day-to-day aspects of running a business, with referrals and leads not always followed up as consistently or thoroughly as they should be.

Most business owners know they should do more to get more referrals; they just don't have time to do it. In other words, **it's common knowledge, not common practice.**

A Great Referral Strategy Starts with a Great Attitude!
OK, now that you understand the "why" behind referrals, how do you actually get them? The short answer is always the same – you must ask for them.

In reality, most business owners know that they must ask for referrals to get more referrals, but the *fear of asking* impedes them from moving forward. Fear is rooted in your attitude. Meaning, if believe that you are putting your customer out by asking them to give you a referral, then you will never get past the fear of asking.

But, if you truly believe that by asking them to give you referrals, you're helping them, then your fear will fade quickly. Your customers *want* to give you referrals. In fact, a recent study found that 91% of clients would give a referral but have never been asked – that's just amazing!

People like to give referrals because it makes them feel good to know that they've found a great resource and can share their "little secret" with their friends. In many ways, sharing this information shows them to be someone "in the know." And, when a customer receives great service, the result of a friend's recommendation, both you and your referring customer feel the benefit of doing a friend a great favor.

The 6 Easiest Ways to Get Quality Referrals

Over the years, I have tried, created, and implemented many referral programs. What I am going to show you now are the fastest, easiest, and least expensive way to get referrals for your business.

I use these methods in my own business and recommend them to clients who want to increase their sales as soon as possible in the most efficient and quickest way possible. Some of these ideas may sound simple. But often, simple works the best.

Let's take a look...

1. Ask, Then Follow Up.
I didn't say it was complicated or not obvious, I said it was easy. If it's that easy, then why don't more people ask? First, they don't know how. Second, they feel awkward asking face-to-face. For many people, asking for a favor is uncomfortable.

So, what do you do then? Ask using greeting cards. Sometimes getting a referral can be as straight forward as sending your best customers a referral-marketing card. On the other hand, you should be asking for referrals on just about every letter or postcard you send out. Asking for the referral can appear as an "after thought" and therefore, is seen as less threatening to the reader.

Remember, **don't ask if you're not going to follow up.** In most cases, if one of your customers went out of their way to give you a referral, they're eventually going to ask you how their contact worked out. People feel good when they help a friend, and it makes them feel important to be considered as someone "in the know."

So, don't disappoint (1) the referral giver, (2) the referral (who might be expecting you to contact them) and of course, don't lose an opportunity to make another sale.

2. Thank Your Customer for Giving You a Referral.
Referrals are magic, powerful, and completely free. Therefore, you should feel obligated to personally thank each person who took the time to give you a referral.

If you treat your customers extra special after they've done a great service for you, expect to receive more referrals from that person in the future. By thanking your customer, you reinforce why he or she feels confident to refer your business in the first place.

3. Send Greeting Cards That Get Attention & Make People Smile.

I love sending cards that make people smile while thinking about my business. But cards don't always have to be about buying something. Sending out interesting or funny birthday cards shows your "human side" and helps your customers get to know you, like you and trust you more.

If your card is unique, it may get passed around to others, which only increases exposure for your business. To get referrals, you need to stay "top-of-mind', and sending cards help you do just that.

4. Implement a 'Thank You' Card Program Throughout Your Company.

When was the last time you received a thank you card for something...anything? If you're like most people I speak to, it's been a while. When you did receive a card, how did it make you feel? Probably pretty good.

My point? Sending thank you cards will get you noticed because nobody else does it. And you can bet that not only will it make the person receiving the card feel great, but guess who they will recommend when your product or service is needed? YOU!

There is always a reason to thank someone for something. Encourage every person and department in your business to send thank you cards, from the shipping clerk to the cashier. Your business will reap the benefits.

5. Give Referrals to Businesses You Trust.

Want to get more referrals? Then give more referrals. That's the "give to get" method. The "law of reciprocity" says that when you give something to someone, they feel obligated to give back. That works extremely well when it comes to referrals.

But rather than just calling and reading the information over the phone or sending an e-mail, I send cards. Why? A card is remembered longer and makes a bigger impact on the person getting the referral. Not only did I give a valued business a great referral, but I also took the time to send them a card with all the contact information on it. That's powerful and something very few people do.

6. Become a Valuable Resource.
How would it make you feel if I sent you some free information or valuable resources that you could use to grow your business? I'm not talking about a "quote of the day." I'm talking about books, magazines, articles, etc. that would teach, inspire, and motivate you and your employees.

Few businesses today do this. But you can, and you should if you want to remain "top of mind." Remember, people prefer to do business with – and refer business – to people they know, like and trust. Do something to stand out and you will get yourself and your business noticed. Become a trusted resource by sending valuable information, and you can make this happen. The "Law of Reciprocity" pays big dividends.

Improve Your Customer Service & Get More Referrals

Listed below are a variety of easy ways to improve your overall customer service, gain repeat customers and generate referrals.

The 12-Point Customer Complaint Checklist.

1. Say I'm Sorry
2. Listen and don't get defensive or argue
3. Empathize and respect their perspective
4. Don't make excuses
5. Understand the problem by listening and asking questions
6. Tell them how you're going to fix it
7. Tell them when you'll get back to them

8. Thank them for complaining
9. Resolve the problem
10. Tell them it's resolved
11. Do something extra nice for them…NOW!
12. Continue to stay in touch (postcards, newsletters)

11 Things You Can Do to Really Make a Difference.

1. Smile – when greeting a customer in person and on the phone, always smile.
2. Use Age-appropriate Greetings – avoid referring to older customers and women as "guys".
3. Be Proactive – ask how you may be of service.
4. Stay Visible & Available – never hover.
5. Avoid Answering the Phone Via a Speaker – it may be convenient for you, but it shows you are doing something else at the same time.
6. Don't Avoid Your Customers – Don't turn away, walk away, start to make a phone call, or duck beneath the counter as a customer approaches (we've all had it happen to us).
7. Limit Personal Calls – make personal phone calls only when on break and out of earshot.
8. Never Say, "I Don't Know" – unless you add, "but I can find out for you".
9. Aim to Please – if a customer wants something that isn't on display, go to the stock room and try to find it.
10. Be Time Sensitive – don't let chatty customers monopolize your time if others are waiting
11. End Every Interaction Pleasantly –smile as you're saying goodbye and encourage the customer to come again.

9 Great Customer Service Ideas.

1. Greet Every Customer – even if you're with someone else, take a moment to greet a new customer and tell them that you'll be right with them.
2. Return Phone Calls as Soon as Possible - rapid return of a phone call lets customers know how important they are to your business. Don't let 30 minutes pass without returning a phone call whenever possible. (I know this is a hard one)
3. Same Day Service - If you have something that your customer wants, consider promising them same day service and go the extra mile to deliver it.
4. Owner Visits - If something goes wrong after a purchase, as the owner, call them to try and make it right.
5. Send Special Gift Packages - when a customer invests in a high-priced product or service, send them a customized gift package.
6. 90-Day Survey - perform a customer satisfaction survey 90 days after purchase. Start your phone call with, "Our service starts after the sale, so we're calling to check up on you".
7. Check & Clear Voicemail – do this daily to avoid missing important messages.
8. Check E-mail Daily – even a quick reply is better than no reply.
9. Birthday Marketing – want to really stand out? Implement a birthday card marketing system.

The Wonderful World of Customer Reviews

Let's face it, nobody is going to buy a $10,000 hot tub, a $30,000 swim spa or a $50,000 inground pool before they check out your company's reputation. And where do they go do that? The Internet of course.

Having plenty of high-quality reviews from a variety of review sites can make the difference in a prospect buying from you or your competition.

The Value of a Great Customer Review

Positive customer reviews are golden. They build trust, garner attention and can help overcome skepticism even with the toughest buyers. Reviews are "social proof" and third-party endorsements. One of the best things about getting great reviews is that they will help you close sales forever!

According to research released from a Bright Local Online Review Survey:

- 84% of people trust online reviews as much as a personal recommendation.
- 54% of people will visit the website after reading positive reviews.
- 73% of consumers think that reviews older than 3 months are no longer relevant.
- 58% of consumers say that the star rating of a business is most important.
- 94% of consumers would use a business if they had at least four stars.
- 100% of consumers would consider a business with five stars.

*https://www.brightlocal.com/

These statistics prove that you need to get more reviews, more frequently and with higher star ratings.

Despite the popularity of reviews, many sites frown upon, or even forbid, incentivizing customers for reviews. Google and Yelp have issued the following statements regarding this practice.

- Google: "Don't offer, or accept money, products or services to write reviews."
- Yelp: "Don't ever offer freebies, discounts or payment in exchange for reviews."

So, if you can't incentivize customers to get reviews, what are some other ways that you can obtain them?

Provide Extraordinary Customer Service.
The first is obvious. You want to provide the best possible customer service. That alone lends itself to getting positive reviews. Of course, if you always do what you say you're going to do, you're easy to do business with, and you show customer appreciation, reviews will come naturally.

Ask for a Review or Encourage Satisfied Customers to Write One.
Another way to get reviews is to simply ask for one when someone says something good about your company, products, or services. If you get a text, e-mail or phone call from a customer thanking you for a job well done respond back and ask if you can use their kind words as a review or testimonial. Even better, you can suggest that they go online, select their favorite review site, and leave an official review.

Put a Reviews Procedure in Place and Share it With Your Staff.
Next, you need to coach your staff on what they should do when a customer says something positive. You need to have a procedure in place for your employees to use when somebody compliments any aspect of your business. This procedure should specify how your staff should document the compliment and where it should be submitted for a review.

In addition to creating a reviews procedure you need to train your staff on when to ask for a positive review and how to respond to a negative review.

Make it Easy for Customers to Leave a Review.
The next business strategy is to make it easy for people to recommend your business through a positive review. Develop an automated reviews system and add it to your website. Then, when someone has a complement or wants to say something nice, you can direct them to your website's "Reviews Tab."

Here's Why You Always Need More 5-Star Reviews

You may be thinking, "Why do I need more reviews? I already have 73, or 86 or 143 5-star reviews." The answer is, no matter how many reviews you have now, it's never going to be enough.

In the BrightLocal survey cited already, they asked local consumers how recent does an online review need to be to be relevant? A whopping 69% of respondents said within two months!

Clearly, you need to get new, updated reviews regularly. The fact that you have 143 reviews is good, but if they are over 12 months old, they are not as effective as they could be.

Let's look at the restaurant industry as an example. If you visit Yelp to check out a restaurant that you have never been to before and they have 100 reviews, your initial reaction is "that's great."

But, if you dig deeper and see that the most recent reviews are two years old, then you may think twice. Often, in the restaurant business at least, ownership, menus and chefs change frequently. Any one of those things could have occurred in a two-year period. Therefore, you need to constantly be getting more reviews to remain current and fresh.

Multiple Review Site Ratings are a Must!
In many cases, businesses tend to get reviews from one particular site like Google and stop pursuing reviews on other sites.

BrightLocal asked consumers how many different review sites they visited before making a decision about a business. 79% of respondents said they look at two to three online review sites.

While there are many online review sites and industries differ, here are 3 important sites:

- Google™
- Facebook™
- Yelp™

Here are some review sites for home improvement or contractor businesses:

- Houzz™
- HomeAdvisor™
- Angi™

Whichever sites you select, just be sure that they are popular with your customer and prospect base.

The Importance of Yelp and Google My Business Reviews.
As of this writing, Yelp feeds reviews to Bing, Yahoo and Apple Maps. Yelp is important not only because it's an authority site, but because it also feeds the Bing and Yahoo search engines.

If you have reviews coming from other sites, they may show on Google's Knowledge Panel Listing (rich results that show up on the Google search engine page). The more varied your review sites, the more likely that Google will find one or more sites to import.

The Best Time to Ask for Feedback.
When is the best time to ask for a customer review? The answer depends on what you want to get reviewed.

If you want to get feedback about your sales process, then asking at the time of the sale would be best. On the other hand, if you're looking for feedback about how much your customer enjoys their product, then asking for a review within the first 30 days would be best.

Why 30 days? New buyers are most likely to use their new product more frequently and are the happiest in the first 30 days after purchase.

If you are a service company, or just want to get more reviews about your service department, asking for feedback right after a service problem is resolved makes sense.

When a customer says something positive by phone, in the store or via email.

Train your staff to recognize positive feedback and to ask the customer to turn that positive remark into an online review. And, if the customer agrees, to let them know you are going to send a friendly reminder e-mail.

The one thing *you don't want to do* is set up a "reviews station" in your store. Review site algorithms are sophisticated, and they will see that all your reviews are coming from your store IP address.

Using Surveys to Solicit Feedback.

When it comes to surveys, the first rule is to keep it short. Only ask questions that have a specific purpose.

Here are a few good questions to ask:

- Was the product was delivered on time?
- Did the service person answer all your questions?
- Did the service person go through the instructions?

Other Things to Consider.

- Ask questions that can help you improve the products or services that you provide.
- Don't ask multi-part questions. It can be confusing for someone that's filling in the survey.
- Use checkboxes to make it easier to answer the question.
- If a person can just fill in a "yes" or "no" question, it's more likely the survey is going to be answered.

The other great thing about using a survey is that it can lead to a review. Rather than asking for a review, you are asking for feedback using the survey form.

At the end of the survey leave a place where someone can enter their name and give you a 1 to 5-star rating. Most people will naturally continue filling out the survey form and give you a review.

How Positive Reviews Can Improve Search Results

Yelp, Facebook, Google My Business and other reviews sites now show your average star rating. There's no question about it – star ratings can help you stand out and get clicks.

According to a BrightLocal survey, listings with five stars earn 69% of the clicks. Listings with four stars earn 59% of the clicks. The more Google reviews you have, the more likely it is that you are going to appear in the Google maps "three pack." When your listing does appear in the top three, reviews become a major factor affecting your click through rate.

The Effect of Reviews for Your Business.
Professor Michael Luca from the Harvard Business School published a study, which demonstrated that a one-star increase in ratings equals a 5% to 9% increase in revenue.

Although his study concentrated on the restaurant business, one can infer that the higher your star ratings are the more traffic, leads and sales you will get.

TripAdvisor did a study that found that when a hotel was able to move their ratings up one-star they could increase their room rates by 10% without affecting occupancy at all.

The Hidden Benefits of Customer Reviews - User Generated Content (UGC).

The obvious benefits of getting positive customer reviews are things like increased sales, more online visibility and hopefully more website traffic. But there are some hidden benefits of customer reviews.

Dealers are always trying to come up with new ideas and content to keep their website fresh and relevant. The great thing about customer reviews, is that it is user-generated content or UGC – in other words, you don't have come up with content yourself. Satisfied customers are doing it for you and it's free!

Not only that but reviews also give you real news that you can share on Facebook and other social media sites.

Another hidden benefit of these UGC reviews is that you can "repurpose" them into video testimonials. This takes a "one dimensional" written review and turns it into multi-dimensional video review that can be seen and heard.

Check out some video testimonials on my website: **https://spapoolmarketingsuccess.com/**

Now, you can now take those videos and upload them to sites like YouTube, Google and Facebook as well as adding them to the testimonials page of your website. The great thing about posting these videos is that it helps you stand out in the search engine results because most search engines still show a little video "thumbnail" photo which leads to higher click-through rates.

Here's the Problem - Traditional Ways of Generating Online Reviews are Ineffective.
Traditional ways that dealers "ask" customers to leave a review is just by adding a "Review Us" button somewhere on their website. Although this is certainly "better than nothing," it is a very passive method, and the results are usually meager at best.

The Dealer Automated Reviews System (DARS)

There are two types of reviews in the Dealer Automated Reviews System (DARS).

- 1st Party Feedback left and displayed only on your website and

- 3rd Party Reviews left on review sites like Google and Facebook which are independent of the business.

Website visitors are either encouraged to go to your website's Reviews Page or find it on their own. The Reviews Page serves two purposes. The first is to show visitors reviews left by others satisfied customers.

The second is to have a place where customers can leave a review – either positive or negative. Once the reviewer fills in the form, the DARS system takes the review through the follow up funnel that correlates with the review. If the review is a 4 or 5-star positive review they are taken to a Thank You Landing Page.

On the Thank You landing page they will see a video that thanks them for leaving their feedback and asks if they wouldn't mind taking it one step further by clicking on their favorite review site that are listed on the page.

If they do click on one of the review links, they are taken to the review site where they can copy and paste the review they just left. Now the review is published on the Google or Facebook.

Even if the reviewer decides not to click on one of the links, the DARS system will automatically publish the review as a feedback or a website review. Additionally, if the reviewer does not click on one of the review links, the system will automatically send them up to three follow-up emails encouraging them to leave the review on their favorite online review site.

Normally, the first e-mail goes out the same day the feedback is given. The second email is scheduled to go out 24 hours later. Then, the third email will be sent 24 hours after that. However, you can change the timing of when the e-mails are sent out.

Only a total of 3 emails are sent. If they haven't responded after the third e-mail, most likely they are not interested in doing so.

"Apology" Landing Page.
For negative reviews, which are those receiving between a one to three-star review, they are taken to an apology landing page.

On this page, there is a video spokesperson who apologizes to the reviewer. It explains that though there are systems in place to provide the best customer service, unfortunately this time something went wrong and that a company representative will be in touch with them shortly to try to resolve the issue.

There is also an additional form on the Apology Page where the reviewer can leave more details about the issue and reviewers are given the opportunity to leave a review on Facebook or Google.

Shortly after the customer leaves their negative review, the DARS system will automatically send you a notification that someone left the review. However, the negative feedback is not published on your website.

The reason it is good for you to see the negative reviews is to help identify issues that you may not be aware of and allow you to fix them before the problem gets worse. It gives you the opportunity to contact the customer, find out what the issue is, and make it right.

The Initial Set Up of the DARS System.
During the initial set up of the DARS system, all 5-star reviews from the major review sites are imported and shown on your website Reviews Page. Moving forward, any new 5-star reviews left on the review sites like Google and Facebook will be continually imported to the site.

The DARS Backend Dashboard.
The DARS system comes with an online dashboard where you can control how the system operates. Other than the reviews stats, one of the most important features is the ability to send out requests for reviews and feedback.

Companies that have the most success with this program are those that are proactively using this feature, and not waiting for people to leave a review. Additionally, you should upload any new customer e-mails to the DARS system and begin to create separate lists by product line, services, or any other beneficial parameter.

Once you upload your e-mail list, the DARS system will automatically send out a series of up to 3 follow up emails requesting feedback. You can send these emails out 3 days in a row or spread them out.

Conclusion.

Whether you use the DARS system or not, the bottom line is that you need to:

- Get more and better reviews
- Get reviews from more sites
- Systematize the review process
- Train your staff on how to get reviews

To learn more, check out the following website:
www.DealerAutomatedReviewsSystem.com

Post Pandemic - Learning from the Past, Building for the Future

First it was 9/11 and then the Great Recession. With each new "crisis" came a change in consumer buying habits. Now with Covid-19, I think consumer buying habits have changed even more dramatically.

Six months after 9/11, consumers had the money and motivation to open their wallets and buy. Although some dealers were negatively affected, by the end of 2002, the pool and spa industry had recovered nicely.

During the great recession (2008-9), hot tub sales plummeted, many dealers went out of business and there was a lot of industry consolidation. Large manufacturers bought struggling brands and got bigger thereby increasing their market share.

Once again, consumer buying habits changed. The new normal then? Many people still had money to spend but were more reluctant to do so. Savings rates increased and readily available information on the Internet made consumers smarter and better negotiators. In addition, there were fewer buyers in the market and dealer "year over year" sales increases were smaller if they increased at all. I remember a common saying during the recession was that "flat is the new up" meaning that dealers felt lucky if they had a flat year versus a sales decline.

The dealers that did survive the recession and eventually thrive did so because they adjusted to the "new normal." They got smarter by upgrading their websites, Internet marketing strategies and overall lead generation techniques.

Interestingly, social media sites like Facebook, Twitter and YouTube really came "of age" during this time. Pool and spa dealers who were "early adopters" of these new technologies gained a huge competitive advantage to reach out and interact with consumer in a totally new way.

Now, as we look back at 2020 and 2021 no matter how good or bad you were at marketing and promoting your business, you probably sold out just about anything that had to do with keeping kids and families occupied at home during the pandemic.

And although we were one of the fortunate industries that "benefited" from the Pandemic, I don't want us to get complacent. I believe the change in consumer buying habits is more dramatic and permanent than those from 9/11 and the recession. Because of that, you need to be thinking about the new and different sales and communication strategies you'll need deploy to satisfy the needs of all you current customers and future prospects.

So, let's talk about what we can learn from the past and how we can build for the future.

Why Were Some Dealers More Successful During the Pandemic?

I have reviewed dozens of websites and stats from Google Analytics, Google Search Console and Google Business Profile. The goal was to try and find out why some dealers were more successful than others and reveal the strategies that would help explain their success.

My first observation is that dealers that had already invested in high quality and consistent marketing and implementing systems and automation were better prepared than others to weather the dramatic change in the economy and the marketplace.

To put it another way, dealers that were more successful in 2020 and 2021 already had effective websites, Google placement and systems in place to follow up, so when the pandemic hit and the floodgates opened, they were much better able to handle the influx of leads. Now, there were still new strategies they had to learn like Zoom meetings and virtual tours, but those were much easier to implement than setting up entire lead generation systems and follow up.

To summarize more specifically, dealers that were more successful during the pandemic already had…

- A highly visible presence on the Internet (Google, Bing, Yahoo)
- An informative, easy to navigate website
- Systems and automation in place to maximize lead generation <u>and</u> follow up
- More communication options for consumers – better, faster, and more convenient
- Online shopping options

Based on these findings, here are 10 Internet marketing strategies that successful dealers are using now to capture more leads, follow up more easily and ultimately close more deals. Because many of these strategies are inter-related, you'll notice that a few strategies like CTAs (calls to action) or adding an online store are mentioned in different categories.

1 - Stay Visible Online and Add a Lead Gen System - There are more prospects now searching the Internet for hot tubs, swim spas, saunas, and pools than ever before. Internet traffic based on Google Analytics stats is up 20-40% depending on the dealer – that is huge! People that were "stuck at home" or are still working from home are using the Internet to keep up with the news, stream movies and buy products remotely.

But traffic alone isn't enough. Traffic without leads won't generate sales or pay the bills. Dealers that have high quality lead generation and follow up <u>systems</u> in place are taking full advantage of this increased traffic and continue to grow their business.

<u>Recommendation</u>
- Make sure you have an "end-to-end" lead gen system in place that includes online advertising, website calls to action and automated and human follow up.

2 - Offer an Online Store – Customers and prospects need to maintain their hot tubs, swim spas and pools and need chemicals and water care products. Dealers that have an active online/e-commerce store where customers can purchase what they need from home have been generating more sales in the last year than ever before. I have one dealer that sold almost $4000 just last week alone!

Recommendation
- Stop putting it off – get your online store done now, then start promoting it. If you're like my other clients, it will more than pay for itself and increase your cash flow almost immediately. Woo-Commerce, Shopify and PayPal are just a few sources that can help you do this.

3 - Have a "Better" Website – In this case better doesn't mean prettier, better means better/more ways to engage with customers, better calls to action (CTAs) and better user experience (UX). Other than "contact us" and "request pricing", what CTAs are on your website? You need CTAs for every part of the buying cycle – before and after the sale. Better UX means, faster, mobile friendly and getting visitors where they want to go in the least number of clicks.

Recommendation
- If you already have CTAs on your site, are they the right ones? Do they appear on every page? Do they all have an automated way of following up with the prospect? Do they automatically get added to your newsletter list? All of this is not hard to do, so ask your inside marketer or agency to get it done.

4 - Add or Update These Popular Pages on Your Website – Based on the stats that I'm tracking the most popular website pages are:
- Home - obvious
- Promotions/Sales
- Used Hot Tubs
- Contact Us
- Online store

<u>Recommendation</u>
- Make sure your promotions page is up to date – NEVER have a blank promotions page
- Add a Used Hot Tubs page to your website if you don't already have one and add some photos and pricing. Even if you rarely have used tubs to sell, add the page.
- Have multiple ways for customers to contact you – email, phone, Facebook messenger, chat, and text
- Create an online store as soon as possible

5 - Communicate Better and More Often – What's the best way to communicate with a customer or prospect? The way <u>they</u> want to communicate, and the more options you can give a prospect, the more likely it is you'll generate a lead and start a conversation.

As dealers, we obviously want all prospects to pick up the phone and give us their name, phone number, model selection and of course credit card. But the reality is that only a small percentage of prospects will ever do that, at least on their first interaction with your company. And since a high percentage of customers and prospects will visit your website before they interact with you, the more options you give a prospect to contact you the more likely it is that they will. So, it just makes sense to offer a variety communication options such as:

- Website Chat
- Facebook Messenger
- Facebook Chat Bots
- Text via a mobile phone
- Phone
- E-mail

In addition to incoming communication options, you should also be using outbound communication. Have you been sending our newsletters to your e-mail list?

Another critical form of outbound communication is using your Google Business Profile (previously called Google My Business or GMB). Google has added the following attributes that you can update to your Google Business Profile, which appear in Search and Maps. This includes:

- curbside pickup
- no contact delivery
- delivery
- in-store shopping
- same day delivery

Recommendation

- If still appropriate, make sure your website is up to date in terms of days/times you are open and a reminder about all the services you provide.
- Start sending out regular e-mails and newsletters and not just about sales and promotions
- Add additional forms of communication options to your website

6 – Deploy More Effective and Better Marketing – Stop selling and start marketing! Remind your prospects about the benefits of owning a hot tub, swim spa or sauna. Staycations are back in style and being more health conscious is more important than ever. All these products can promote family fun, togetherness, and improved health.

Recommendation

- Write and promote blogs about staycations and how owning a hot tub or swim spa can keep the kids "busy" while improving over health and well-being. I recommend video blogs because they are interactive and can be used more effectively for cross channel marketing.

7 – Integrate Better and More Consistent SEO – Reviewing stats from Google Analytics, Google Search Console, Google Business Profile as well as some paid SEO tools, I have seen a huge increase in the following keyword searches – Used Hot Tubs, Hot Tub Sale and Hot Tub Sale Near Me. These are not new keywords, but the number of searches for them has dramatically increased.

Recommendation
Check your ad and analytics stats for popular "non-company branded" keywords. Then be sure to incorporate these keywords into your on-site and off-site search engine optimization strategy.

8 – Don't Stop Advertising - In times like these, your competitors will slow down or even eliminate some or all their marketing efforts. This creates an opportunity for you to capture their customers and increase market share if you already have strategies and systems in place to do so. Your job is to take advantage of this opportunity and find those prospects that are ready, willing, and able to buy and make sure that they buy from you, not your competition.

Recommendation
The fastest way to generate traffic and leads is Google AdWords. But don't be fooled by how easy it is to get started. AdWords can be a huge "money pit" if you don't set it up properly, monitor and optimize campaigns effectively.

75% +/- of all clicks on Google come from non-paid/organic search results. This includes Google Business Profile, website clicks, YouTube videos, press releases, images and more. What is your organic search strategy?

9 – Promote and Master Virtual Selling – There is a huge difference between selling a prospect who is sitting in a dry hot tub in your showroom and trying to sell someone online via a virtual tour. Even your best "in-person" salesperson may need to learn some new skills to sell online.

Recommendation
- Make sure you have the right computers, laptops, tablets, and mobile phones to be able to conduct online meetings – do they all have cameras?
- Make sure you have the right software – Zoom, Join.me, Skype, Facetime, Google Duo
- Be aware of your surroundings – the noises you can't hear around can be very distracting to person you're talking to or "Zooming" with. This includes background music, people talking, running spas, wind, and rain, etc.
- Practice, Practice, Practice – Try selling spas to each other online and then helping each other get better

10 - Offer and Promote Financing – Not a new concept by any means but making sure every prospect knows you offer financing is a good idea. Get creative if possible and practical. "No, No" financing has worked effectively in the past (no interest, no payments).

Recommendation
Make sure you effectively showcase your financing in all your sales communications - website, newsletters, etc.

Conclusion
If 2020 and 2021 has taught us anything it's that a "new normal" has arrived. Online shopping will increase even more as consumers get used to the convenience and "safety" of "click and ship" shopping. This doesn't mean customers and prospects will stop coming to your showroom, but it does increase the importance of increasing your online visibility and availability. If you want to survive and thrive in the coming years, you'll need to spend more time, money, and resources improving your overall Internet marketing capabilities.

How Critical a Role did Systems and Automation Play for Successful Dealers in 2020 and 2021?

I think those business owners that already had proven systems in place to help run their business, sold more, stressed less, and were able to handle more leads than those that didn't. For those dealers that didn't have automated systems to follow up properly, when the pandemic hit, they were over-whelmed and timely communication just got worse

The problem is that sometimes, when sales are good, it can mask some of the inefficiencies that dealers and manufacturers have. It can minimize a lot of things that should be improved. But in "super-charged" sales years like we had in 2020 and 2021 these inefficiencies can hurt dealers short and long term, even when sales are really good.

Systems and processes are important because they're consistent, repeatable, and predictable – and they clearly define who does what and when.

For those dealers designing customer and prospect follow up systems, please be sure that everyone involved knows the following:

- Who's in charge of following up with leads?
- What are they supposed to do when they get the lead?
- What happens if you have multiple salespeople?
- How do you measure and monitor the progress of that success?

With Demand So High Now for Hot Tubs, Swim Spas and Saunas, is Advertising or Marketing Really Necessary?

The short answer is a resounding YES!! When prospects typed in "Hot Tubs XYZ City" and your company did not show up on page one, it meant that they had to really work hard to find you. The fact that you got any of that business at all is only because of the overwhelming demand for hot tubs in your area. But those dealers that were on page one once, twice, or even three times, got those leads and eventual sales well before dealers whose website didn't appear online until page 2 or 3.

Think of it this way... "Pandemic buyers" shopped the same way pre-pandemic hot tub buyers always did - the sales process still happens the same way. They sat in a hot tub somewhere (i.e., a neighbor, hotel, resort, or gym), and they went home and husband and wife or partner said, "Why don't start looking for a hot tub?"

And where did they start that search? They went to Google and typed in "hot tubs" or "spa sale near me" or whatever it was. And they still researched the same way. So just because your sales have doubled from year to year, doesn't mean you couldn't have sold a lot more!

The pandemic created a "once-in-a-lifetime" opportunity to grab market share and introduce your company to thousands of prospective customers. So, keep marketing and advertising. Don't blow it.

What do Pool and Spa Buyers Expect Now from Dealers?

Expectations at the factory, dealer and consumer level have definitely changed. There are things today that consumers are expecting from dealers that they were more tolerant of before the pandemic. Buyers now want to be able to find what they're looking for even quicker on the Internet and expect faster response times from sales and service. Consumers today now are comparing your company not just to other hot tub dealers, but to the best service at premium brands like Apple, Nordstrom or even Amazon.

Dealers need to step up and meet the expectations of a more demanding and more educated consumer. That's why an improved user experience at every stage of the buyer journey needs to fit the lifestyle, shopping convenience, and delivery speed of their prospects and customers.

So, how do you turn these market and buyer changes into opportunities to grow your business? I suggest you start by reviewing specific buyer expectations. Some are the same as they were before Covid-19 like good customer service while others like curbside pick-up, didn't even exist 6 months ago.

Here is a list of 7 things that pool, spa and sauna buyers expect now:
1. Finding what they're searching for faster on their favorite search engine
2. Locating current and reputable sources of information they need to make informed buying decisions
3. Faster response times from sales and service
4. Better and more varied forms of communication that fit their needs, lifestyle, and time frames
5. Improved shopping convenience and delivery speed, both online and in-store
6. Worry-free and easy-to-navigate websites and e-commerce stores
7. Buying with confidence

Let's go through each expectation in more detail:

1 – Finding what they're searching for faster on their favorite search engine

With more people working from home, Internet usage and shopping from home has skyrocketed. People are spending more time searching the Internet for products and services than ever before and that includes pools, spas, saunas and many other backyard or indoor exercise, health, or family entertainment options.

That's why it is more important than ever that your business show up on page one of Google. Although, I've used these stats earlier in the book, they are worth repeating. According to some studies, up to 90% of people searching for products and services on the Internet never search beyond page one. That means that for all practical purposes, if you're not on page one, your prospects will never find you! And if they can't find you, they can't buy from you either.

Although there are many strategies that you can deploy to help you achieve page one status, I suggest you concentrate on these 4:

On-Site SEO
On-site search engine optimization (SEO) are the things that you do on your site or to your site to make it easier for the search engines to find your business. On-site SEO involves implementing a lot of little things that over time add up to something much bigger. It can involve optimizing your site for specific keywords and updating titles and descriptions to be sure that you are telling Google what every page on your website is about.

Organic Off-Site SEO Internet Marketing
Off-site SEO many times referred to SEM (search engine marketing) involves inbound Internet marketing strategies using properties other than your website that you manage like YouTube and Facebook. SEM can also involve press releases and directories like Houzz. These strategies are designed to appear in the organic section of the search engine results, and in some cases can rank high for months or even years, I suggest that dealers move some their PPC budget into these organic strategies.

Pay Per Click Advertising (PPC)
Creating an effective Google AdWords campaign can not only get you to the top of page one within an hour, if done correctly, can help you drive more traffic to your website and generate a ton of leads. Understand however that PPC does not help your organic rankings and your ads will stop showing as soon as your daily budget is used up (another reason to do organic off-site-seo).

Google Business Profile (previously called Google My Business)
Optimize your Google Business Profile page with a powerful description, generate more reviews, update photos and videos and post regularly. Doing this will not only improve your chances of ranking higher in the "3 pack" but directly affects your Google Maps listing and your Google Knowledge panel (the vertical description of your business that appears on the search results when you type your company name into Google).

2 – Locating current and reputable sources of information they need to make informed buying decisions
Don't make the mistake of devoting all you content development to just creating ads. Ads attract "now" buyers found at the bottom of the sales-funnel, which is obviously important, but what are you doing to attract future buyers just looking for information at the top of the sales funnel?

Education Based Marketing (EBM) is about helping prospects or customers better understand something, while engaging them just enough to find out where they are in the buying process. EBM reduces fear and distrust, establishing a relationship that encourages a willingness to buy. The more you educate your prospect, the more you build a relationship of trust and respect, the more likely they will take another step in the customer journey.

Buyer's guides, stats, blogs, infographics, and videos are just a few types of information you can provide to prospects to help them better understand the benefits of using your products and services.

3 – Faster response times from sales and service

In today's hyper-competitive market, responding quickly is essential. Responding in real time via phone or chat is ideal and always preferred, but the reality is you can't always do that and run your business at the same time. When real time responses are just not possible, using automation to bridge the gap is critical.

Prospects requesting simple information like brochures and buyer's guides can easily be handled using a Call to Action (CTA) form on your website that automatically sends them a download link using an autoresponder. Autoresponders like Infusionsoft, Mailchimp and Emma can handle this for you.

Using an automated chatbot is another great tool for providing requested information and answering questions on your website and Facebook. Answers to frequently asked questions (FAQs) can be pre-written and delivered when asked using a chatbot. Good chatbot strategies always give the user an option to call or message the business directly.

Using autoresponders and chatbots can get prospects some of the information they need quickly while freeing up your time to handle other aspects of your business.

4 – Better and more varied forms of communication that fit their needs, lifestyle, and time frames

I already wrote about this in the last chapter, so I won't dwell on it here. Just remember, the best way to communicate with a prospect is the way they want to communicate, and the more options you can give a prospect, the more likely it is you'll generate a lead and start a conversation.

5 – Improved shopping convenience and delivery speed, both online and in-store

Savvy retailers are making it easier than ever before to cater to the wants and need of today's buyers. So, if you want to compete, you need to adapt as well.

Ever heard of BOPIS? It stands for "Buy Online, Pick Up in Store". In addition to BOPIS, there are other buying adjustments you should consider. Take your que from retailers outside the pool and spa industry and see what they offer. Some of these ideas include:

• Special hours for seniors, first responders – open 30 minutes early (grocery stores are doing that)
• Free Delivery – just set reasonable distance limits
• No touch/curbside pick-up – the buyer pulls up to your store front, calls you, pops the trunk and you drop in the water care or accessory products

6 – Worry-free and easy-to-navigate websites and e-commerce stores
Stop putting it off – get your online store done now, then start promoting it. If you're going to start selling products, services, and accessories online, you'll need to have a secure website to accept payments. This means https versus http. Talk to your webmaster on what is required to get this done.

Speaking of e-commerce, you may want to consider additional forms of payment other than traditional credit cards, cash, or check. This includes things like PayPal and Venmo.

7 – Buying with confidence
Other than price and salesperson, what criteria do prospects use to decide to buy from you versus your competitor? It usually comes down to product warranties, after the sale service and of course dealer reputation and reviews.

Product warranties are mostly set by your manufacturers, but after sale service and reputation are things that you can control. Great dealers know that having a responsive and well-trained service department is critical, so I am not going to spend any time writing about that here. What I will concentrate on is improving your reputation and generating more 5-star reviews.

Let's face it, nobody is going to buy a $15,000 hot tub, a $30,000 swim spa or a $50,000 inground pool before they check out your company's reputation. And where do they go do that? The Internet of course.

Having plenty of high-quality reviews from a variety of review sites can make the difference in a prospect buying from you or the dealer across town and no matter how many 5-star reviews you have now, it's never enough.

From what I've seen, most dealers don't have a formal system in place to either ask for or promote reviews. Traditional ways that dealers "ask" customers to leave a review is just by adding a "Review Us" button somewhere on their website. Although this is certainly "better than nothing," it is a very passive method, and the results are usually "ok" at best.

I suggest that you implement a system to help you generate more reviews. The past several years has seen a variety of review system "pop up." We developed the Dealer Automated Reviews System (DARS) (https://DealerAutomtedReviewsSystem.com) for our clients and it has been very effective.

Conclusion
The pandemic has already changed the way consumers buy products and services both online and in-store. Your customers now expect more buying and delivery options as well as faster service. Dealers that "get" this and adapt quickly will generate more sales today and gain continued loyalty well into the future. Implementing systems and automation can help you achieve your goals faster and more efficiently all at a nominal cost.

Closing Comments

I hope you were able to read through the entire book and more importantly pick up some ideas to help drive more traffic to your website, generate more leads and ultimately increase sales.

The next step is to take action and get started as soon as possible. Remember, good intentions don't increase sales.

No need to try and do everything you've learned all at once or by yourself. Pick a few strategies and get started. See how long it takes and measure the results. Satisfied? Do a few more.

Not satisfied with the results or just spending too much time implementing? Then I would suggest that you select the most important strategies you want to complete and hire a professional to get it done. This will free up your time to do what you do best – closing sales, delivering products, and enjoying your free time!

To your continued success!

Ready to grow your business?

Discover how to drive more traffic, generate more leads, and increase sales using our proven strategies.

Just visit our website:
www.SpaPoolMarketingSuccess.com

or call David Carleton directly at:
858-442-3131

Success Stories

Every year, we select a vendor of the year that has most impacted our business. The 2012 Vendor of the Year went to Dave Carleton!

We have been using Dave for our Internet Marketing since 2009. From social media, to SEO to video marketing and Google AdWords, Dave seems to do it all and do it well.

He keeps up with the latest in Internet marketing strategies and continually presents us with new strategies that he has already tested.

Dave doesn't hold you hostage like so many other Internet marketing companies do. Instead of holding back on his knowledge and experience, he empowers and educates us. Dave does steady and solid good work.

Every year, we select a vendor of the year that has most impacted our business. The 2012 Vendor of the Year went to Dave Carleton!

Want to increase sales and get your business on page one of the search engines? Just call Dave.

Sue Rogers – Oregon Hot Tub

I am pleased to report that traffic and sales have increased. I credit Dave's hub and spoke marketing strategy

We have made only one major change in terms of marketing in the last 3 months – we hired David Carleton from Spa Pool Dealer Success to upgrade our Internet marketing efforts. We decided to focus on my Minneapolis stores, and I am pleased to report that traffic and sales have increased. I credit Dave's hub and spoke marketing strategy.

What I like about Dave is that he takes the time to explain his strategies, solicit our input and then executes as promised. In addition, Dave has made himself available to answer my questions even on weekends when most "traditional" marketing agencies are closed. If you are looking for an "out of the box" approach, personalized attention, and proven results, then call Dave.

Thad Schaben – Hot Spring Spas of Iowa and Minnesota

Traffic & sales are up, we rank either #1 or #2 or both on dozens of keywords on Google and we continue to grow our business.

I have hired David to do a variety of projects over the last few years including Search Engine Optimization, video marketing, other internet marketing strategies that I don't want my competitors to know about. The results have been great.

Traffic and sales are up, we rank either #1 or #2 or both on dozens of keywords on Google and we continue to grow our business. I have told David that whenever he develops a new Internet marketing strategy, if he recommends it, then I want to do it. Dave is reasonably priced, honest, and over delivers on his commitments.

I highly recommend David to any online or "bricks and mortar" business looking to grow their business.

Phil Sandner – Easy Spa Parts

Due to Dave's efforts, we now appear either #1 or #2 on page 1 of Google for our targeted keywords in both hot tubs & pools.

I have been working with Dave Carleton for the last 9 months or so and have been very pleased with the work he's done.

Dave did a great job optimizing our website which had fallen almost completely off Google.

Due to Dave's efforts, we now appear either #1 or #2 on page 1 of Google for our targeted keywords in both hot tubs and pools.

We know for sure his strategies have helped us generate leads and were able to track many of these leads to closed sales. Dave is honest, easy to talk to and really wants us to succeed.

Dave makes himself available at all hours of the day including weekends. Dave is very transparent on all the work he does for us, no "smoke and mirror" double talk like many Internet marketing companies.

In addition, he takes the time to explain what he is doing, why he is doing it and what results we can hope to achieve.

If you are looking for a true Internet marketing professional, that knows the pool and spa industry, then I highly recommend that you call Dave Carleton.

Tom Junck – Combined Pool and Spa

About the Author

David Carleton is President of SpaPoolMarketingSuccess.com and specializes in showing spa dealers and pool builders how to spend less and get more from their marketing and advertising using low-cost strategies in local business marketing, lead generation and conversion, Internet marketing and social media.

Dave was Vice President of Dimension One Spas for 6 years where he developed sales; marketing and training programs that helped hundreds of dealers in 30 countries around the world generate leads, increase sales, and enhance their overall marketing effectiveness.

Dave has been a keynote speaker for many industry, Chamber and trade groups across the United States and has written several manuals including The Ultimate Lead Generation System and The Essential Referral Marketing System.

Dave also created a podcast devoted exclusively to the industry called **The Spa Pool Marketing Success Podcast**. **Listen and Subscribe for free** – Now Available on Apple iTunes®, Google Podcasts, Spotify, Amazon Music, iHeart Radio and many more.